ISBN 978-0-9567599-0-0

Find You,
& You Find Everything:
The Secrets to the Law of Attraction

The 'Raw' version
The pre final-editing version of this book, including signature
and quotes compilation exclusive to this edition.

Hemal Radia

ADDITIONAL CONTENT

To receive additional content, go to:

www.HemalRadia.com/FindYouContent

Hemal Radia website

www.HemalRadia.com

Manifesting & Law of Attraction blog:

www.ManifestingandLawofAttraction.com

You can also find content from Hemal Radia on various social networks and websites such as Facebook, Twitter, etc.

ABOUT THIS VERSION OF THE BOOK

Since word spread that this book was being written, there have been many enquiries about it. The intention in releasing this Limited Edition 'raw' version is so that this information is available as soon as possible to those that are wanting it, and that they can enjoy an exclusive edition of this book.

So, if you see any typos or anything that does not quite appear or sound as you might expect, I encourage you to defocus your attention to that, and take in the overall essence of this book, which is really what it is about. In doing so, this book and the essence and vibration within it will benefit you powerfully

I encourage you to focus on the essence and vibration of this book. That is, and always will be, the most important thing in anything.

There are some quotes at the end of this book which have been compiled exclusively for this version.

TESTIMONIALS

Just the chapter on Abundance was way better than The Secret and The Power put together; it was simple, practical and very realistic. A blind man can read it and be amazed!
Narda Mohammed, Life Coach, New York, USA

The DEFINITIVE guide to changing your life with The Law Of Attraction! You have the knack of understanding and explaining the principles of Law of Attraction, for example, way better than Abraham and Esther Hicks. There is no better text on this subject — this may be the most important book you will ever read. Hemal Radia is a master teacher who explains the Law of Attraction and the power of manifesting better than anybody else, and in terms everyone can implement instantly.
Lena Mitchell Jasiak, Perth, Australia

You are amazing. You are, in my opinion, the world's leading expert on Manifesting and the Law of Attraction
Wendy Franklin Muhammad, Host of Authentic You radio show, Chicago, USA

Thank you Hemal!! I love your work and the way you word your teachings. You are by far my favourite Law of Attraction teacher!! Keep up the good work!!!!
Gillian Gregory, Elgin, Scotland

Finally... a book that explains the Law of Attraction in terms that everyone can understand. Whether you are new to the concept of LOA or if you have been practicing LOA for years, everybody will benefit from reading this fabulous book. Hemal explains the science behind LOA, how it works, and how to apply the techniques to your life. If you are ready to create the life that you have always dreamed of for yourself, this book is a must!!
Rebecca Perry, Atlanta, Georgia, USA

You are the only person that made me truly understand "The Secret"...seriously! I am really practising! Everyday, I'm doing it properly - since I met you. I always think that something big is coming my way...and I am enjoying the absolute now. I always find something to be happy for. This is AMAZING, THANK YOU!! There is not one day that I do not think how grateful you have made my heart. Thank God you exist, Hemal!!
Silvia Bardellini, Ibiza, Spain

This book is full of wisdom, has more knowledge, is more practical, and is easier to understand than all the other books I've read from other Law of Attraction experts. It also has the sign of a good book that as you learn and take in more, the more you read it. More was manifesting in my life even the day after reading Hemal's book. Thank you so much Hemal for the results, alignment, joy, and master-class knowledge of this book!
S Patel, West Midlands, UK

You are a brilliant beacon of light and wisdom, Hemal. In my opinion, no one brings it like you in the Law of Attraction business. Thank you for all you do.
Peter Ruble, USA

If you are wanting results, Hemal is the perfect person. He will give you the perfect answer....and you're always left feeling really good.
Stephanie Swann, Arizona, USA

You are SIMPLY THE BEST! Thank you again, Hemal. It means A LOT to me. I wish you success and happiness, always. You are loved.
Claudia Caecilia, Indonesia

I love the way you are so effortless when you talk about the Law of Attraction, unlike so many other speakers who almost make it sound like something incomprehensible. You are doing much good Hemal! And I feel really blessed to have connected with you.
Georgina Laros, Personal Development Coach and Author of "Tables & Chairs", South Africa

Thank you for sharing your wisdom with the world!
Karla M Nashar, Indonesia

A wonderful inspiring book that highlights everything we need to accomplish our dreams is already within us. Learning to let go of fears, to trust our inner voice and align ourselves naturally to universal energies really does attract people and events into your lives. The book is extremely easy to read and follow for anyone interested in accomplishing a life of health, happiness and abundance. Highly recommended!
Angela Mahandru, Editor of "Choice - Health & Wellbeing" magazine

Once again, Hemal has used his extraordinary ability to explain the mechanics behind the so-called 'Law of Attraction' in very simple and logical terms, while paying particular attention to one of the most often overlooked aspects of the subject - vibration! This book is a must-have for readers seeking a greater awareness of our inherent power to consciously create our deepest desires.
Derek Smith, North Carolina, USA

Hemal brings the principles of Law of Attraction to life, making them easy to understand and incorporate into your daily life. He brings a practical and 'easy' approach, making it a pleasure to work with him! I'd recommend Hemal's book to anyone looking to learn Law of Attraction and find joy, peace and abundance in their life!
Peter, Sydney, Australia

I've listened to feel-good music and I've seen feel-good movies; tonight I read a feel-good book! Direct with its message, as well as clear in its guidance, Hemal's book will help you close the gap between the current you and the you, you want to be! If you want a feel-good life, this book can show you how.
Carl 'The Barefoot Broadcaster' Munson

This is truly wonderful. You have a real gift in how you say and bring these laws across for people to really grasp. Thank you so much, for sharing your gift with us!
Cheryl Corson, USA

Some rise to the occasion, and some are just like you - THE Occasion.
Thank you for being you. Your presence adds an extra pulse to
my everyday consciousness.
Tammy Tran. USA

Hemal has an INCREDIBLE handle on the laws of vibration. The
chapter on Abundance alone was filled with so much insight that it was able
to give me an entirely new perspective. You must read this book,
it will change your life!
Justin MacArthur Rand, Light Beam Academy, Boston, USA

Keep touching the world, you are young, gifted and amazing.
Laura Tynes, USA

The special thing about Hemal Radia is that he helps us remember how
special WE are.' 'Hemal takes the 'thinking' out of the Law of Attraction
and puts the feeling and flow back into it. There is no reason why any of us
can't be a master at our own lives after reading this book.
Fran Stockley, UK

This book is AMAZING!!! Hemal Radia's genuine Spirit and passion to
teach others THE LAW OF ATTRACTION comes straight from the
heart. I've listened, read, and used his techniques. The result, LIFE
CHANGING ideas and inspirations, SELF LOVE and getting in
touch with the SPIRITUAL side of myself PURE POSITIVE
ENERGY & knowing that I AM A DELIBERATE CREATOR
of my life's experiences. He has taught me to harness the power of my
thoughts. My vibration continues to climb daily and I am excited about
how I have become a vibrational match to all my dreams and desires. I
know that there is nothing that I CAN NOT BE, DO OR HAVE.
Once you pick up this book and implement his teachings in your daily life, I
PROMISE, YOU too will see INCREDIBLE MIRACLES
MANIFEST ALL AROUND YOU.
Thank you Hemal for manifesting your beautiful SPIRIT & teachings
into my life. NAMASTE.
Linda Lypchak, Healer & Self Help Inspirational Student Miami,
Florida, USA

You are amazing at what you do!
I just read the next chapter and I'm hooked! I am LOVING this.
Hemal's divine writing style allows me to truly comprehend the Law of
Attraction. His writing engages me and his use of visualization really
defines the point and expresses the truth behind the Law of Attraction. He
has a talent for writing in a way which touches the spirit. After reading
this, I feel more in tune with myself and my journey. I am going to read this
every morning as a jump-start to my day!
Candice Quinn, Scottsdale, Arizona, USA

APPRECIATION

Thank YOU for your asking for this book. For every creation there is a corresponding asking through vibration. Thank you for YOURS.

Thank you to my family who many years ago might have wondered about the journey I was on. I imagine everything makes sense now.

Thank you to my good friend Brad Meyer. It has been a wonderful journey and with so many exchanges, inspiration, and pearls of wisdom shared both ways. Thank you for all the wonderful exchanges.

Thank you to Georgina Laros for the wonderful friend that you are and our interactions. You are a constant beacon of light for all around you. Thank you also for letting Oprah know about me!

Thank you to Angela Mahandru for your diligence and the sharing of your expertise for this book, as well as your excitement about it.

Thank you to Stephanie Swann for your support in me as a person as well as in the work that I do. Thank you for your faith in me. It is no less than the faith I have in you and in the extraordinary person that you are.

Thank you to Jessica Smith for your friendship and expertise over the years. Thank you for excelling at both.

Thank you to Hilory Wallk for being such a wonderful friend and for wanting the world to know about me. You are an inspiration and are doing a wonderful job in sharing all you do through your sites and resources.

Thank you to Bhavini Raicha, Lena Mitchell Jasiak, Rebecca Perry, as well as so many of you – I appreciate you <u>ALL</u> - who have been excited and in anticipation for this.

Thank you for your excitement, encouragement, and appreciation of this book. *You* have played a part in this too. There are no coincidences.

CONTENTS

INTRODUCTION

In recent years, the "Law of Attraction" has become more and more popular. It could be said that it is due to the various products and books that have been released. It could also be said that these products are *as a result of a growing consciousness and awareness.* It can only happen as a result of a vibrational match and for a calling for it. *Thank you for your calling for this book that you are reading.*

There is no coincidence you are reading this book. Something comes into our lives when we are ready for it.

This book will clarify and demystify "Law of Attraction" for you. You will understand Law of Attraction like you never have before. You will understand that it is really about the harmony that you have within you that affects your own vibration, which affects what you attract into your life. As you change your signal, the Universe - via the Law of Attraction - responds accordingly to you.

After reading this book, you will more clearly understand this dynamic relationship between you and the Universe. You will be able to better understand the thoughts and emotions that you have, and have had, that have led to what has happened, and is happening.

This book will explain Law of Attraction in a very 'pure' sense. There is much material out there which tries to mention the Law of Attraction though which include many non-essential aspects which are not necessary in understanding and mastering the Law of Attraction. *This book will look to explain Law of*

Attraction in the most pure way and without diluting it with aspects which are non-essential.

Enjoy the experience of this book. *Not only will you be taking in the information from the book on a conscious level, it will be working with you on an unconscious level as well as a spiritual and vibrational level. It is not about the words that you read, it will also be about the transformation within you.*

Do not be surprised if by the time you finish this book, that things start happening in your life. Coincidences and synchronicities happen, manifestations occur, things 'release' themselves, and you feel more of a connection to everything else.

Do not be surprised if there is a lightness within you before the end. Also, in your understanding of the dynamics of the relationship that you live in within this Universe, there may be a sense of peace and a knowingness that all is well. From this book and any subsequent others you will understand the dynamics in play in your life and in others in your life.

This book has been titled "Find You, and You Find Everything" because it truly is about who you are. You will discover what this means as you journey on the trail of light beautifully arranged by this book. As you discover more about yourself, you will find that your connection to everything that you want is so much more pronounced. *You will find that everything that you want is ready to enter your life and it just requires you being in tune with it, and the best way of doing that is in being in harmony with yourself.*

Whilst the subtitle of the book is "The Secrets to the Law Of Attraction", the Law of Attraction *has always been available to you.* Throughout the ages, various doctrines, disciplines and cultures have believed that there are 'secrets' to the Universe that are being withheld from you.

There are no true secrets. You receive whatever you are resonant to. You are an aspect of the Universe and it has always been willing to share anything that you ever wanted to ask it, and it always does. This book will just reveal those 'secrets'.

You will learn perspectives and viewpoints about your relationship with yourself and the Universe which will greatly impact your life and in you getting all the things that you want. *If you know that 'secret', you know it all. Find You, and You Find Everything.*

The path already exists and it is perfectly formed. When you are on it, you know by the joy that you experience.

19

SOME OF WHAT YOU WILL FIND IN THIS BOOK:

- Realise who you are on a deeper level and tune more into YOU

- You do not need anything else, other than yourself

- Tune in to YOUR divinity, YOUR magic

- You will understand the structure of the Universe and your relationship to it

- You will understand exactly HOW you are attracting the things that you are wanting and how the Universe brings them to you

- You will understand the part that actions play in this whole manifesting dynamic

- You will know more about your flow and how to tune in to it

- You will understand about the flow of money and abundance

- You will get into tune with the meaning of love that resonates for you

- You will remember things that have not made sense in the past, and you will understand the deeper underlying causes and how they make more sense now

- You will be reminded of your connection to everything else and how your desires are sovereign and priceless and not only an expression of you, but also an expression of the Universe

- You will learn nuances and perspectives which will improve your manifesting abilities. They will allow you to be more in tune with who you are and with the things that you want, so they flow more easily into your life

- You will understand the Law of Attraction better than you have done before

- You will learn and be reminded of the significance of your emotions and how they give you all the information you want to know

- You will be reminded of the true abundance and infinite potential around you which is YOUR birthright

- You will remember and realise the infinite and abundant possibilities for you

- You will realise that you have known all of this. There is no coincidence that are holding this book in your hands. It is reminding you of who you truly are.

- You will remember that you are a divine being and all possibilities and creations are open to you.

This book will give you information about You, the Law of Attraction, and Manifesting that you may not have been consciously aware of. It will broaden your perspective about yourself and the world around you and the possibilities within you. It will *remind* you of your possibilities and of You.

Because, when you Find You, You Find Everything...

ABOUT HEMAL RADIA

Hemal Radia is a world-renowned expert on Manifesting, Law of Attraction, and spirituality. He has shared his insights and worked with people from all around the world for over 15 years. He has guided clients, attendees of his events, and readers of his material, to their dreams. In addition, his quotes on the Universe, Law of Attraction, Love, your Flow, and many other topics, have inspired many thousands worldwide.

Over the years, Hemal studied and synthesised information on creation, the Law of Attraction, Manifesting, spirituality, and much more. He identified and worked with the underlying principles to create his own tools and techniques and apply them in his own life. He shared this information and these perspectives to enable others to more quickly and effectively be in tune with what was important to them and who they really were. They would experience manifestations and wonderful flows that they could not have believed before.

There is no coincidence in you having this book in your hands.

We look forward to the wonderful journey ahead together ...

FIND YOU, AND YOU FIND EVERYTHING: THE SECRETS TO THE LAW OF ATTRACTION

The "Law of Attraction"

The Law of Attraction is a universal law and is prevalent everywhere. It is essentially that *"like attracts like"* - *from a vibrational perspective*. This last caveat - "from a vibrational perspective" - is important.

Many times, people think they are focusing on something though they do not attract it and believe that Law of Attraction does not work. The reason for this is because the overall vibration of the thoughts they were having were not resonant to the vibration of what they were wanting.

Everything in this Universe has a vibration on a deeper level. In fact, 80% of the objects you see around you are 'space', but they are vibrating so quickly on a deeper atomic level that they appear as solid.

Your thoughts are also of a vibration, as are your emotions. *As you think about something and keep your attention on it, you attract more thoughts of a similar vibration*.

As you think a thought and keep your attention on it, you attract another similar thought. And *as you continue to keep your attention - vibration - on something, you attract more thoughts.* As this continues, the 'mass' get larger and larger and the attraction and pulling power gets stronger.

You then feel this physiologically. There is a growing excitement building within you (Assuming that this is something positive that you are focusing on. Law of Attraction works for everything, positive, negative and everything else), *you feel it in your emotions and this is an indication of your vibration.* Your emotions are a preview to what is coming in your life.

Soon enough, you experience things not just physically in your own body, but *you start to see synchronicities and 'coincidences' around you.* You may manifest what you have been thinking about - something that is a vibrational match to it - or you may attract various coincidences and happenings on the way towards it.

As you offer a vibration to the Universe, by universal law – i.e. there are no exceptions - it offers you experiences that match that vibration. The Universe offers you an "echo," so to speak.

It is a Vibrational Universe That You Live In

This is a vibrational Universe and everything is organised and orchestrated through vibration. When many people try to understand and learn the Law of Attraction and struggle with it, it is because they are looking too much, or only, at what they can 'see' and do not have an awareness and understanding of what is unseen. In this book, you will learn more about the unseen, including the energetic and vibrational dynamics between you, your desires, and the Universe.

Another reason why people do not attract the things that they would like is because they offer a mixed vibration. We mentioned above that when someone thinks a thought and focuses on that thought, they attract more things that match that vibration. But what happens for many people is they do not cleanly focus on something. *They think thoughts contrary to that thought.*

So for example, they may want to be in a relationship and feel good about it, but then have thoughts about loneliness or of fearing being in a relationship. Someone may think about money, but then focus on what it feels like to be without it. These all contradict the original desire and hence there is not much movement.

If you offer a mixed vibration to the Universe then you will either see mixed results or not very much movement. It is like trying to drive a car whilst having your foot on the brakes. You are offering resistance to your flow.

You will learn more about vibration in subsequent chapters. Like vibrations attracts like vibrations.

"Find You, and You Find Everything"

Whilst there is this universal all-powerful law called Law of Attraction that is accessible to all, the way that *YOU use it in your life is through the signal that you offer to the Universe through your vibration.*

This is why the emphasis of this book is in finding your divinity. The Law of Attraction has always existed and will always do so. *What happens in your life will be as a result of what you 'put out' vibrationally.*

It is about your relationship with yourself and who you are on a deeper level, which you will learn more about in this book. *As you get more and more into alignment with that, Law of Attraction will magnify that alignment and you will see it in your manifestations.*

YOUR ABUNDANCE IS HERE, AND ALWAYS HAS BEEN

The Abundance You Desire is a Magnification of the Abundance you Have

Abundance is a favourite topic for so many who want 'more' in their lives. After all, as you will discover in this book, *expansion is something that is very natural to you.*

Many look at the lack in their lives and are blind to all the gifts that exist in their present moments. They look outside of their now for something else, and forsake all the true 'richness' that is already existing in their now moment.

In realising the abundance that is in your life, more abundance finds its way to you.

In having ones attention to what is wrong, or how things are not perfect, they offer a vibration of dissatisfaction. And of course, if they are offering that vibration, how can what they want enter their reality when it is a different vibration? It cannot. *If you are offering the signal and frequency of dissatisfaction, satisfaction, prosperity, and abundance cannot enter your life – it will not be a match to the signal.*

You attract matches to the vibration you offer.

27

It is by realising your true abundance in your now, that you access the abundance that you are wanting. By your attention to what you DO have, you offer the vibration of attracting more.

You may say: "Oh, but I don't have abundance. How would I get it?" The answer is by finding things you *can* appreciate in your life. By noticing the things that you *do* have, you offer the vibration for more.

It's not what you have, it's the vibration you offer about what you have, by your attention to it.

Do you have the ability to feel like a millionaire with what you do have? If you are single (or even if you are not), can you feel love within yourself as if your soulmate is already in your life? If you want to develop your body, can you FEEL as if you have that body? That is what it is about. It does not matter about which context, it is about your ability to live and embody what you want within you. The Universe cannot resist or deny that and by universal law, your physical world reflects your inner world.

The Universe can provide you all that you want, but you have to be offering the signal for it. Through your vibration, you have to be saying to the Universe: "*I am already that. And if I do not have the physical manifestation it will be fine because I KNOW I am it.*" This is a very strong signal and the Universe cannot resist it. It has to provide the manifestation.

Abundance is an inherent quality of the Universe. It exists in every iota and every molecule in all that is. When there is lack, it is due to the *resistance* of the natural abundance that is available and flowing through everything that you see around you.

28

Abundance exists in every aspect of the Universe; it is an inherent quality of the Universe. When someone says that they do not have it, it is like standing on a small desert island and saying there is no water. Have your eyes adjust to the water, and notice it all around you

As you will realise from this book, you are not just a physical being but also a divine spiritual being that is connected to everything else. All possibilities exist for you and you are not separate from that which you want.

The Universe does not limit you or constrict you. Only you can do that through your own beliefs and attitudes. You have freedom in this Universe, other than that which you withhold from yourself.

Prosperity and abundance are inherent in everything and are available to you through your activation of them through your vibration with your thoughts.

Abundance is Being in Tune with your Birthright

For many, "abundance" is something that they are seeking in their lives. They usually mean it to be money or financial wealth. We can expand this definition to include that aspect of abundance - money, as well as remind you of all the other abundance that is with you and always has been with you. *You are truly a prosperous, abundant, and divine being* and will be reminded this as we continue.

This book is a reminder of who you are. Everything is within you. This book will reconnect you through your allowing of it.

29

Abundance is not just financial abundance. If you have money and only money and nothing else, you might be fine for a while, but without flow in your life it would soon be difficult. You are not a being of acquisition, but a being of flow. The acquisitions are a consequence of your flow.

Life is not about the acquisition of things but about flow and movement. It is not about having a pile of 'things', without the lifeblood of flow and wellbeing. 'Things' soon deteriorate without that connection. Though with flow and wellbeing, the 'things' will naturally accumulate as a consequence of your flow.

Money is a physical example of abundance, but it is not the only form of abundance in the Universe. Abundance is more a quality, a trait and aspect of the Universe, rather than a specific 'thing'

Abundance is being in tune with your natural birthright.
From that place, you have access to all that you want.

Abundance is beyond money; money is an expression of it. You can have money, and not necessarily abundance. There are people who have money that have lives that are out of balance and live fearful lives – this is not what being in an abundant flow is about. *See it as a way of being, than a way of having. The having is as a consequence of you 'being'.*

You can have abundance and not 'need' money, but know that you will be taken care of, and you will.

30

Abundance is With You and Around You All the Time

As we were saying, abundance can have a broader meaning than just physical possessions - although there is nothing wrong with them, just that abundance can mean more than them. The word itself also means "limitless" and "plentiful."

Abundance can apply in all contexts and areas. We can be abundant in relationships, have abundantly healthy bodies, and have abundance in all the other areas of our lives. Abundance has more to do with your universal flow rather than a specific 'thing'.

You are never separate from your flow. It is about tuning in to your magical, natural, ever-present flow.

Rather than it be a 'form' (such as money), have abundance be more to do with your flow. *It is more of an infinite and unlimited nature, rather than it being a 'form'.* People often focus on the physical – much like with most things in life – and do not see the non-physical or spiritual aspect of it. *Abundance is to do with your energetic flow, which leads to the abundant physical manifestations in your life.*

Everything has a non-physical or spiritual component behind it. In fact that part is so much greater; just like with an iceberg you do not see the majority of it which is 'beneath the surface'.

Prosperity in your life as physical manifestations is a consequence of prosperity in your consciousness.

31

When you are truly connected to your flow, you will find the right things showing up at the right times. Oftentimes the solution will be there before the 'problem' appears - not that you will see them as problems because you will be too busy being in your flow.

Abundance finds itself to you via the path of least resistance determined by your thoughts and beliefs.

There are No Limits, Other Than Those That You Create

The Universe, and you on a vibrational level, are expanding eternally. There is no limit to this expansion. It is *eternal and infinite*.

Some people have beliefs that for them to have what they want, they feel that they are taking from someone else or that there is "only so much". This is a scarcity perspective, rather than a thought from a prosperity or abundant consciousness. There is absolutely no limit to your growth or acquisition in this Universe. *You are never taking from anyone else because they have their own source, as you do, and there is an infinite supply for all.*

You may have thought that there is a limited physical supply of things. But *through your vibration and flow, there is limitless creativity* and ability to create physical resources. *There are infinite possibilities as to what you can create in this physical world. The possibilities are only limited by your perceptions, thoughts, and beliefs*. Namely, your vibration.

32

<u>Your Alignment Enables Your Allowing of</u>
<u>What You Want</u>

What you choose to see, you will see more of. What you choose to 'ask' by your attention to it, you will get the answers to, and a match to it in what you experience and see.

There are no limits to what you can create. It comes through the alignment of your vibration, which comes from envisioning and thinking and believing from what you want.

When you have a goal or desire or something that you want, it has already been created in spirit – that is why you are having a desire for it. It then just takes you *aligning your beliefs and thoughts with it for it to come into your life*. This is 'alignment'.

When you are aligned to your desires you will be feeling magical – even if the manifestations have not come yet – and in your flow. When you are in this place within yourself, it will feel very exhilarating as you will be aligned to the spiritual aspect of you and in synch with the Universe.

The key indicator is how you feel. The manifestations may be occurring also, or on their way – they are a confirmation rather than an early indicator (although they can be that too).

Alignment is being, thinking, living, and knowing as if your goals have happened and not needing to check, because you know you are living them.

What limits you have, and have taken on to believe, have come from either what you have learnt from others, or from limitations you perceive in the physical world. When you realise

33

that the physical world is a projection and manifestation of your consciousness and vibration, and there is an infinite world within you, your possibilities open up.

Realise you are a child of the Universe, an expression of it; no separate or different from ALL the other miracles within it. You are as deserving as every other aspect of it.

Abundance is as ever-present as anything else is in this Universe. It is pure potentiality. It IS the Universe. The Universe is a fertile ground for your creations and your expansion.

If the Universe is a fabric, abundance is one of the threads that it is made from, along with threads such as pure potentiality, infiniteness and other inherent qualities.

The Universe, and you, are full of pure potentiality, and all possibilities.

There are More Possibilities Than You Can See

Your now moment is as rich and abundant as you see it to be. Seeing the abundance in it, shows you more.

There are many ways abundance comes to you other than only through the form that you call 'money'. **When you think something can only come to you through one path, you are limiting the ways the Universe can deliver to you what you want.**

34

The Universe's possibilities are unlimited and infinite, your conscious mind's logical and rational notions are limited and finite. But using your conscious faculties, you can determine your vibration, through which you communicate with the Universe, and enable it to deliver what you want. That's the way it was intended to be. *You let go of the 'how', let the Universe take care of that, and you focus your thoughts and vibration on what you want, and how good it feels.*

Through our economic upbringing we have been led to believe that money is almost the *only* way we can have what we want. I want to remind you that is not the case, *the Universe has many more ways of delivering what you want to you,* exactly what you want.

Through society, economies, and beliefs we have picked up along the way, we see only the physical and economic model. Realise there is a deeper, vibrational existence and reality. The physical and economic model is a manifestation of it. *Change your beliefs, and the world that you see changes.* The possibilities and opportunities change. What comes into and out of your life changes. It is all down to your vibration.

People's belief that money is the only way that what they want can come into their life limits their ability to experience abundance. *They keep looking for money whilst all sorts of abundance is <u>already</u> blossoming around them.*

They keep looking for the money. And as their attention is on the lack of it, they keep seeing the lack of it. *They do not see all the other lavish possibilities happening around them all the time.*

Money too can come to them. But by their attention to the lack of it, and their fixation and attachment to it, the flow is not allowed as well as it can be.

Society and the human race have become attached to the notion of money because it has been believed, especially through our economic systems, that it is one of the only ways to have what you want. This perspective is very much based on what we can see. There is nothing wrong with that. But we are just reminding you there are other avenues *in addition* to that.

There is more around you and within you that is unseen which is the source of the creation of what you see. The power of which is beyond what you could imagine or perceive with your conscious physical notions.

Abundance is an internal thing; external abundance is a natural manifestation of it.

You Already Have Abundance in Your Now

Abundance is not something that needs to be 'created'; abundance is an aspect of the Universe and exists ALL around you ALL the time. It is in the fabric of the Universe.

It is about you tuning in to the abundance that is already around you.

You can be in a sea of prosperity and not see it because you have your vibration and perceptions such that they do not enable you to see it. Or, you could be in a field of poverty but you will be the one whom prosperity chases because you are aligned to it. *It is down to your vibration and you attracting vibrational matches*. If you are not aligned to it, it is much like having the salt cellar right in front of you and not seeing it.

36

You attract that which you are a vibrational match to. Where is your attention in this present moment?

The Universe could be repeatedly showing you what you want but you are not seeing it because you believe it must come through another form, when in actual fact you could have – and have had - what you want a lot sooner. Be open in your beliefs as to how things can come to you.

The Universe Responds to Your Vibration, Not To What you Have or Don't Have

You tune into abundance by appreciating what you DO have. You offer a vibration of abundance and attract more abundance. It becomes easier because as you see more abundance and your attention is on it, you attract more, and so on.

If you are offering a vibration of dissatisfaction, that is a different frequency to abundance. The Universe cannot deliver abundance to you whilst you are offering a contradictory vibration. You would be in vibrational disharmony with abundance.

You may say *"Oh but I don't have a penny to my name! How can I appreciate anything?"* The answer is through your vibration, not through what you have or don't have. ***It is about creating a vibration of appreciation through your focus.***

The Universe responds to your vibration, not to what you have or do not have.

37

Someone who has not even a penny to their name, could find things to appreciate such as:

I appreciate the beautiful sky...
I appreciate the sun shining down upon me...
I love my body and that it takes care of me...
I have some friends I really adore and appreciate...
And so on...

Start somewhere, anywhere, and you will find more things to appreciate. ***It is not about 'what' you appreciate, it is about offering the vibration of appreciation.*** As you do that, by virtue of Law of Attraction, you will see more things that you appreciate, and you will attract and have more things to appreciate. It cannot be any other way, it is universal law that like attracts like.

If you are appreciating, the Universe will give you more to appreciate. And the same is true to the contrary.

Realise the abundance and prosperity that you have in your life today. It is already here. By putting your attention to it you magnify it, and attract more.

It is never about the environment you are in or the context, it is about your vibration. When you change your attention and hence your vibration – irrespective of what is around you - the things in your life change. Either your environment will adapt, or you may find yourself in a different environment - whichever you are most in alignment with.

Your Now is the Path to What you Want

Abundance exists in all places and all the time; it is a matter of whether *you* see it. Look for something in your life that on some level you can appreciate, no matter what it is, the key thing being that you can appreciate it. And make sure that you genuinely appreciate it. Don't force it. Find something that you can appreciate, no matter how small. **The key is your feeling of genuine appreciation**. As you focus upon it, your focus grows bigger, and you notice more to appreciate.

When you are focusing on appreciation in your now, you are channelling universal Source energy through you. The Universe is literally living and flowing through you, in great flow.

Most people are looking for the abundance that they do not see. The irony is that it's about seeing the abundance that they *do* have, and the Universe will match that vibration and give more.

You do not have to chase anything outside of your now. If you see the abundance in your now by focusing on anything that you can appreciate - and put your attention towards it - you will find abundance grow and prosper in your now. **It is always about your vibrational offering in the now.** And you know that through your emotions. The better you feel, the higher your vibration and more 'attractive' you are to all you want.

What many do though is they doubt it. Or they talk about why they cannot have it. Or the misfortune they have had in the past. Or how others have it and they do not. And by doing this they offer a mixed and contradictory vibration, if not a very lackful one. So they draw the abundance, if they do at all, and they push it away also. And so, they do not get to experience what they want to have in their lives.

The irony of it is that you do not have to chase anything outside of your now. If you find something to appreciate in your now and put your attention towards it, you will find that abundance grows, prospers and flourishes in your now.

Positivity and love are additive and attractive and bring together in the Universe. 'Negativity', which is lower on the vibrational scale, separates and divides, whether with others or within ourselves.

When you focus on anything, it grows. When you take attention away, it doesn't, and eventually fades.

Saying that you do not have abundance and asking why do you not have it is like being in an ocean and asking why you are not wet. **There is abundance and prosperity all around you**, all the time. The only reason you do not have it is that with your thoughts and emotions you are not letting it in on some level.

It is like you have resistant beliefs that form an energetic blockage or mesh to prevent universal flow entering. This may be around certain contexts or specific areas; it all depends on your beliefs and your vibration in those specific areas.

If prosperity is available to you, then you may ask why are you not decorated with abundance in all areas of your life? The only way that you cannot have prosperity is if on some level you are not allowing it into your experience with your beliefs.

Your beliefs are your viewpoints on a subject and are your collection of thoughts on the subject.

You are connected to the entire Universe on a deeper level. Limitless abundance is available to you. The only reason something is not present in your experience is if you are not a match to it with your vibration. You are then a match to something else. That is why you have the "something else" in your life, instead.

If you are a match to what you want, it cannot do anything other than be in your life. If you are offering the essence of prosperity or love, for example, it cannot not be in your life.

Be at peace with outrageous abundance. It is your birthright and you can have as much as you want to expect and allow into your life.

How Quickly Something Comes To You is Down To You and Your Thoughts

Being abundant and prosperous is as easy as you allow it to be with your beliefs. ***Your emotions, from your beliefs and thoughts, determine the path of least resistance for what you want to enter your life.***

If you have beliefs that make it difficult to let in what you want by believing it is not possible or having attention to things which are in contradiction of what you want, you will see the manifestation of this along your journey. If you have conflicts about having what you want, then the journey will reflect this also.

The better you feel about what you want, the more in alignment you are with it. If it feels negative or uncomfortable, then there is resistance and conflict of which the emotion is an indication.

41

It is really about the path of least resistance that you have set up by your beliefs. *The more allowing and aligned you are to what you want (by your thoughts matching it), the easier and quicker it is in coming into your life.*

If you are a match to what you want, it will come into your experience very soon. If you are constantly talking or focusing on the absence of it – having a vibration of the absence of it – you will attract the absence of it.

Actions are Easy When You are in Your Flow

People often consider the "actions" they take as hard work and determine how easy or difficult something is by using actions as a measurement. *If you are aligned to something, the actions will be a delight and a joy and will feel less like hard work.* It is about enjoying the journey, and in the process, you are far more attractive to the manifestations also.

It isn't about what you 'do' that determines your journey, it is about your vibrational alignment, your alignment to what you want by your thoughts. That is what will determine your journey; the length of it, and the quality of it.

Things are a lot easier and happen a lot quicker when you are in your flow. And with a lot more fun.

When you are 'doing' things from a place of resistance, it is hard work. It is about being in your flow. When you are in your flow, everything is not just easy, but enjoyable also. You do not think about how easy or hard something is because you are loving it so much. So the question is: how do you find your flow about what you want?

42

How You Create Phenomenal Success

As with any creation, *creating phenomenal success starts with a vibration.* A pure vibration. That is, a vibration with little resistance and attention on what is not wanted, and more attention towards what *is* wanted. This is attractive. And *as there is more and more attention on this, this attracts more, and more, and more, and so on...*

This is how any creation occurs. Whether it be for creating wealth, poverty, sickness, love, joy, happiness. By creating a vibration, not mixing it with thoughts to the contrary, and attracting more and more.

Most people have a mixed vibration, to a lesser or greater degree, about the subject they are wanting to succeed in or about success itself, or something related to either of these. *Once they shift the balance towards what they want, the momentum builds.*

What can then happen is they enjoy their success so much that their vibration becomes even purer – *focusing on the enjoyment and attention to what is wanted and enjoyed – and the momentum gets faster and faster and they attract more.*

What can also happen, is as they get more 'successful', they may experience things which trigger thoughts within them which they do not like. Sometimes even before they have success they may think ahead and start to have fears of what will happen when they are more successful. They may think of scenarios of how others will treat them, or of having less privacy or less time to do the things that they would like to do, and so on. This is an example of a "fear of success." It can be about anything that mixes up their vibration.

43

As they think these thoughts, they bring in thoughts to the contrary of what they want. They are bringing in thoughts of fears and of what they do not want.

Soon enough, they start to see the manifestations of this. If they were previously succeeding, they start to find that the things that were happening for them, do not happen in the same way. Because their vibration is mixed, they do not get the same results that they were previously. They may also start to see things happen which negate their success.

In effect, by bringing this resistance into their vibration, they are sabotaging their success. Of course, none of this may be deliberate. It is by habitual patterns and fears and oftentimes is unconscious, especially at first.

So what can they do about this? Firstly, they can be consciously attentive to their emotions. As soon as they notice that their feelings are not in a positive, joyful state, they can determine what their thoughts are and work on getting them to a better place. For example, they can consciously and deliberately determine what they would like and practice putting their attention on it.

This is what life is about. You progress, you expand, you grow, and you find out more about yourself and your responses to the new experiences that you create for yourself. From these new experiences, you have new desires and new goals to head towards.

Do not think that it is about "making it" to a fixed place, and that will be it. ***Life is an eternal evolution and growth***. It may be the end of a chapter, but there will be another for you, as you are an eternal being. You are far 'bigger' and far 'more' than any goal you could have.

When you reach a goal that you set for yourself, you will have a new perspective that you would not have had before and you will find new things for yourself. It may not necessarily have to be in the same context, but in your expansion and growth, you will have new perspectives.

Living From Your Abundant Possibilities

When many come to the subject of abundance, they often come to it from the perspective of what they do not have. They want to know how to attract more money into their lives and to have the material things that they would like, which is shifting their attention to the positive.

When wanting to attract anything, be sure to be aware that you are wanting to attract it for what it adds to your life, than because of something you do not want. The latter is putting your attention on something you do not want. Make it about what you do want – you attract more of what you put your attention to.

Whilst you can have the material wealth that you would like, it is important to realise that your prosperity is actually much more expansive and broader than that. In you realising that, it also takes the pressure way from your prosperity being only via the means of "money."

Oftentimes, what prevents people attracting more money into their lives is their attachment and "need" to it. Underlying this attachment is an attention and focus on the lack of it - after all, they "need" it. That perpetuates the absence of it further.

45

If you imagine someone on a date and "needing" the other person, the other person will feel this energetically and will feel pushed away energetically as the "neediness" can feel unpleasant. Money, as does anything, responds in the same way. When your attention is on the lack of something and on 'needing' it, you will create an energy around you that is pushing away what you want. Contrarily, if you are in a flow **and from a joyous heartfelt place about your now, you will be attracting and pulling in what you want towards you.**

When you put your attention on the lack of something, you are attracting the lack and pushing away the thing that you want.

People are often looking for abundance which they feel is not in their present moment, rather than focusing on the abundance that they do have. Notice the prosperity that you _do_ have.

It is not important the actual things that you have, but more so your attention and vibration about them. Someone could have limitless prosperity but put their attention on lack, and be pushing away the abundance they have.

Your vibration is determining what you are attracting and pulling in to come into your life next. Someone who has absolutely nothing, can be appreciative, and by their vibration attract things into their lives. **Remember that the world is much more than you see, and your thoughts have access to a level not normally visible.**

Even if you came into this world with nothing, you are a vibrational being and have the ability to attract things into your experience with your vibration. What is physical around you has been created on a thought level first. Most people are not used to their abilities to create in their lives.

46

The easiest place to start to attract what you want is to ask yourself what it is that you want and how you would like things to be. As you focus your attention upon this, and not doubt or contradict it, you will attract more thoughts that match it, and it will grow from there.

Do not limit what you can have by having beliefs just by what you have or have not seen, in the physical world, so far. *You are not just of the physical world, but are also of an unseen non-physical world.*

People limit what they draw from the non-physical by determining their beliefs only by what they see. *If you determine what is possible only by what you see, then you are limiting your potential to only have what has gone before.* You are forsaking all other possibilities – including those currently unmanifest.

Be a visionary. Create the world from your heart and from your possibilities. Not from what only has gone before.

Allow yourself playful abandon to dream about how you would like things to be. Do it for the fun of doing it. Think about those things for the fun of thinking about them and build your thoughts and vibration around them.

As the vibration gets stronger, you will attract more thoughts and start to see the manifestations. This will further your confidence and expectation and allowing of it to come into your life and the momentum will build and build.

When people start to "think" about the consequences and any fears, that is when they disrupt their flow. *Think of what you want from a place of enjoyment, of love, expression, and living as the unlimited creator that you are. See the*

47

possibilities. Create from your place of empowerment, not to "fix" things. Very different vibrations. Assume those things are fixed. Now that they are fixed, what will you create upon this unlimited and infinite canvas that you have? What will you start with today? What feels good to you today? What will you inspire yourself with today?

Abundance is a frequency that you tune into and the Universe orchestrates the details for the manifestation of it. *You do not need to have the answers and need to know the "how."*

You acclimate yourself to that vibration and let the Universe orchestrate matches. That is how it is, and has always been meant to be. *The Universe has always been responding to your vibration.* Are you offering the vibration of the things that you would like coming into your life?

WHAT YOU WANT ALREADY EXISTS: EVERYTHING EXISTS ON A DEEPER LEVEL

There Is A Non-Physical World To The Physical World That You See

You have been so accustomed to the world that you see and hear with your eyes and ears that many have, on the most part, assumed that is all there is.

Beyond what you can see – the physical world – there is a 'non-physical' or 'vibrational' world which is not as easily seen, but more felt and experienced. It is as real and tangible, though not as 'physically' obvious. *It is at least as real and valid as the world you have been accustomed to all your life. In fact, the physical world that you see is a consequence, a reflection, a manifestation of the unseen non-physical.*

Much of what is around you is invisible to the eye but apparent to your heart.

Nothing happens in your physical reality without there being a vibrational or non-physical cause. Many look for physical reasons – because that is all they are used to – but the real causes are vibrational. People may take medication for symptoms or move jobs or countries or change lovers, and find themselves with a similar issue to the one they were moving away from.

They may have changed things on the physical level, but they haven't addressed the vibrational causes. Sometimes

49

changing the physical can change vibration, because it changes our focus, though not necessarily. The important thing to know is everything has a vibrational, or non-physical, cause. *The vibration precedes the manifestation.*

The non-physical and spiritual is around you and unseen as it is vibrating at a different frequency to the physical world you are accustomed to.

Animals hear frequencies that you cannot hear; these frequencies exist even though you cannot hear them. There is a vibrational range at which you experience things through your visual, auditory, and other senses and other ranges at which you do not.

In the case of the non-physical, you FEEL things that are at that frequency. *Your feelings are your guidance to experiencing these.*

There is much more around you that is unseen than is seen. You have access to it through your feelings.

Everything you see around you has a non-physical, or spiritual, equivalent. It is the broader perspective and larger perspective of the physical world you see around you.

The physical world has a sharpness and focus. Much like when you use a magnifying glass to get focus - in the detail there is a focus you would not otherwise have. That is what you are doing in your physical life. You are "on the ground" experiencing physical reality and getting sharper experiences and sensations.

You are a vibrational and non-physical being who came here for the thrill of creating and exploring, that is what you are here for.

50

There is Far More Around You That is Unseen, Than is Seen

You have grown up living a life of what you can see, hear, touch, taste and smell and of being used to believing only what you can see. As well as the physical world around you that you have been aware of, there is an unseen world also that has always existed, and actually, deep down, you have always known.

You have felt it to be the case. Which is what has drawn you to this book. ***There is no coincidence that you have this book and are reading it.***

There is no coincidence for what happens in your life, including you having come across this book.

What you have been taught in school and oftentimes may have been told since then is not to daydream and that what you see is all there is. And to "be realistic".

Your feelings know much more than you can see, hear, touch, taste or smell.

Whilst there IS what you can see and experience with your senses, there is so much more that has been there with you, and everyone else, throughout all time. In fact, ***what you have experienced in your physical world is only a portion of the infiniteness around you.*** Much like when you enter a large park and you choose to focus your awareness in on an area - ***there is much more around you all the time than you have been aware of.***

You are Much More Than the Physical body That You See

Whilst you see your physical body, there is actually a non-physical or spiritual aspect of you that is actually far, far, far more than the body that you see. The body is simply the 'extension' of the non-physical vibration. It is a manifestation of who you are from a larger, broader perspective.

You could even say that this is a magical part of you, but in truth you are ALL magical – all of YOU. This spiritual part of you is connected to everything on a deeper level. When you think a thought, your non-physical, or spiritual, aspect communicates with the rest of the Universe in drawing you towards vibrational matches.

You are a spiritual being having a physical experience rather than a physical being having a spiritual experience.

There is More Leverage in Working With Your Thoughts

People try to create things on a physical level and that is one way to do it, but it is not the most leveraged. Creating through vibration, and alignment of your 'spirit', or non-physical energy, is a far more harmonious way as it is in alignment with you as a physical being, as well as the non-physical being that you are.

Working with non-physical energy through your thoughts and feelings is more efficient because thought is more 'malleable' than something physical. It is more fluid. This is because it is a different vibration. A physical object is a denser vibration whereas thought is a lighter, and more fluid, vibration.

52

When you come to manifest something you work on the thought level, which changes the energy within you, and that affects the things that happen around you. If you maintain and build the vibration and do not contradict it, you will attract things that match it.

There are people that teach Law of Attraction and do not talk about vibration and non-physical. They focus on the actions that you take to "make" what you want without mentioning the non-physical and vibration aspects of the process. This can almost be like using the steering wheel of a car but not turning on the ignition. The spirit aspect of the process turns your ignition on. The actions are a part of steering you to your outcomes. The actions-only approach may work if the ignition is already on and there is alignment, but your vibration is what determines what comes into your life and what doesn't.

Action is best when it is the culmination and consequence of the alignment of your vibration to what you want. *It is you interacting with the physical world enthused with the spirit that you are.*

You Do Not Have to Understand the Law of Attraction For it to Work

You do not need to know about nor understand the Law of Attraction (or non-physical) for it to work because you have been a creator all your life without needing to know the "how-tos". Much like how you do not need to understand electricity to switch your light on, or need to know about the Law of Gravity for it to be working. The laws of the Universe work for you whether you understand them or not. A conscious understanding can be helpful in your approach, but they still 'work', regardless.

The Law of Attraction, as a law of the Universe, works whether you know and understand it or not. That is why it is a 'law'.

However, even if you do not consciously know it, you inherently know all of this. Which is why when you read this book, you will find many things feel familiar. ***Because on a deeper level you know this.*** Our intention here is to remind you of it. To help you find "You" - your 'higher self', 'inner being', 'non-physical aspect', 'spiritual aspect' - whatever you want to call it. You have an inherent awareness of all of this and that is why it may feel familiar. In reading this, you are connecting with You.

If you think certain things and have a certain vibration, you will attract certain things. It is law. You do not have to understand or know how it works.

This is also the same when you are working with others. If you can get them to think a certain way, even conversationally, it will not matter what they believe or if they know about the Law of Attraction. They can even tell you that they do not believe in the Law of Attraction and about attracting things. If you get into a conversation with them and they share their dreams and how wonderful they feel, they are allowing what they want into their lives on a vibrational level. They are experiencing the emotions, and soon enough - if they do not mix up the vibration with thoughts to the contrary - they will feel better and better and find synchronicities happening.

If one is congruently putting their attention to something and they are offering a vibration, the Universe will gladly meet their vibration with examples and situations that are a match.

54

If they are daydreaming about something that they want and are not contradicting it, it is within their vibration and they will attract things that match their vibration.

Someone being excited about something, even if they do not yet fully believe they can have it, just by allowing themselves to get excited, can start the manifestations in the direction of having it. At the very least, it will attract more thoughts of the same and more thoughts and so on until there is a momentum and then there is a manifestation.

What some people sometimes do, when they have a momentum, they bring up their beliefs about the impossibility of it happening and do not feel good about it and block what they want coming into their lives. *But if they daydream about it and create a natural excitement, and do not put any attention to any lack of possibility, they do not create a resistant block and attract a flow towards what they want.*

You and What You Want are Not Separate

There is no separation between you and the rest of the Universe; *on a deeper level you are one and the same.* You are here as an expression of the Universe and as an extension of it for it to experience itself.

This also means that *you and what you want are not separate.* On a deeper level you are very much connected – you are connected to everything there is. You only appear not closer, on a physical level, because of the degree of vibrational alignment you have with what you want.

You are like a drop in the ocean with the ocean being the Universe. You are a part of it and an aspect of it and not separate of it. You are also individual, but again not separate.

There is No Coincidence in You Being Here

You are an aspect of the Universe and an expression of it. There is no coincidence that you are here. *You are living out your dreams, which are an expression of the Universe's, through the life that you live.*

You do not need to question what you want; you are here to follow your desires. The Universe WANTS what you want. It expands THROUGH you.

Your purpose in being here is to follow your joy. That is how you know that you are following your 'path'. There is no pre-set path of specific things to occur, but a direction from the essence of your intention. There are many ways of you expressing this in your physical life. We say physical life, because you are an eternal being well beyond any physical lives. There is no ending, only continuation.

The Expression of Your Joy

The expression of your joy will come in ways in which you can uniquely contribute to all that is. *These ways are unique to you and make YOU special and unique in your contribution to everything else.* We say 'contribution', but that doesn't necessarily imply that you have to be taking actions to help others – in your being a part of this Universe you are contributing to everything there is. If there were not a calling and desire for you, you would not be existing.

You are a unique piece that fits in the larger jigsaw puzzle of all there is.

By you following your joy, you are following the best expression of you and your life here. You are adding to everything else in the best way. The joy is an indicator for you. **It is your connection to the non-physical aspect of you which is aware of the bigger picture for you, your life, and everything else that exists in the Universe.** From your physical perspective you have access to this information when you listen within to your emotions. You have impulses of guidance available to you in all moments.

There is a reason for you being here and with your choices and preferences. You have unique desires and wants, and you are uniquely expressing and experiencing the Universe. This perspective is invaluable and like no other that exists in the Universe.

The Universe doesn't have eyes that will see the Universe the way that your eyes will.

Just like some may like chocolate ice cream and some may like strawberry ice cream. Others may like both together, with nuts. There is a reason for each of you being here with *your* preferences and choices and desires in your life. You have a valuable contribution, and are to be valued and appreciated for who you are. You add diversity to the bigger picture, and more choice on a larger level.

Your desires ARE the Universe's. You are not separate from it but are an expression of it.

When you have a desire, it is also a desire from the Universe. Your expansion is calling you. The Universe wants you to go for what you want; and in your growth and expansion it too expands as a result. There is no coincidence for the desires that you have.

Many people feel that it is not okay to have the desires that they have or they think that they are kidding themselves or 'dreaming'. They may think that they have grandiose dreams and who are they to have such aspirations? **The way you know whether it is ok for you to have these aspirations, is by how you feel.**

When you put aside any doubts and fears and allow yourself to dream, does it feel good? The feeling – whether good or bad – is your indication. Follow what feels good. As you focus upon it, your vibration will align towards it and the Universe will light up your path more and more.

The potential of the Universe is within you. If you look for it, and focus on it...it grows and expands...

When you feel better and better and better, you are more and more aligned with the 'God'/Universe/'Source' (the 'source' of al-that-is) within you. Different people use different terminology when describing the same thing. We will use terms such as the Universe, God and Source interchangeably. **On a nonphysical and vibrational level you are connected to everything and have never been separate, no matter what labels have used to describe the same thing.**

THE WORLD YOU EXPERIENCE IS THE ONE YOU ARE MOST FAMILIAR WITH

The world you experience is not because of the way the physical world is, but because of the choices and observations you have – conscious and unconscious - which create the representations that you have about it. The world that you experience is a total creation.

Your Desires Contain the Mechanics of Their Manifestation Within Them

Just as there are trees within a seed, your desire – within its vibration - has the mechanics for its manifestation.

Your desire is a vibration and within this vibration is an intelligence. Everything is intelligence. Within the vibration of your desire is all that is needed for its manifestation. Your job is to enable the flow of it without contradicting it with thoughts that counter it.

You are a being of the Universe, connected to all the resources of the Universe. How can you ever be denied? All "God's" resources are available to you. You just have to realise them and not doubt or contradict your birthright.

As you put your attention on your desire, and from a viewpoint of feeling as if it is here, you build that vibration. You will see more and more synchronicities and manifestations to support it. Or, sometimes, you may not see any but see the full manifestation of it. *The key is not to focus on what is happening on the physical, but focus on how you feel and your emotions which are indicators of your alignment.*

Focus on feeling and living as if it is in your life. Experience this vividly, and in a very 'real' way. Each time you do this you create a platform for the next thought.

Law of Attraction is that you attract more thoughts and 'things' which are a match to your vibration. As you congruently put your attention to something, you enter the infinite stream of consciousness towards more of it.

Some people have heard that it is good not to have desires. There can be several reasons that they might believe this:

- They have heard that desiring is a state of 'wanting' - i.e. a state of not having and by having the attention on 'not having' they are perpetuating this.

- That desires are not spiritual and are 'ego' based.

There is a Difference Between 'Wanting' and 'Pining'

Regarding the first point above about 'wanting', some would say that this can be like a state of 'pining' and when someone pines for something it is not good. Yes, a state of pining or of this type of 'wanting' (and it is not what we would be meaning when we use the word 'wanting' in most of this book) perpetuates more of the same. *Notice how it feels – that is what it is attracting more of.*

So let us make the distinction between desire, and a state of 'pining'. **Desire is feeling good about the things you would like.** Pining, is thinking about things one would like and having a discord about them, generally because one feels they cannot have them – and this would be down to their beliefs.

If someone starts with a desire and it is from a place close to pining, it would be a matter of working with their beliefs in imagining this reality in their life. **It would be moving towards feeling it more and more in their life, seeing it possible, and building the bridge – in their thoughts – from the original desire, to one where they become very familiar with it.**

As they feel more and more familiar with it, this will be an indication of them aligning their vibration to this reality of them with their desire, and thus they would be closer to the manifestation of it.

So there is nothing wrong with a desire, but if one is pining or focusing on an element of lack, it is due to their perspective and beliefs not yet being quite in alignment with them having it.

'Being' and 'Feeling' Your Goals Versus 'Thinking' Them

Regarding desires not being spiritual or them being 'ego' based, it depends on what one defines as 'ego'. If they are meaning it to be a physical world perspective in determining desires, that is what your physical world perspective is for. If you were only to have a spiritual or non-physical perspective, you would have stayed only as a non-physical being! **You came to this world to have physical experiences and desires and to flow energy from your non-physical perspective.**

You came on this physical plane to have desires which would stimulate you to expand and grow and acclimate to these new directions. You didn't come to have no desires. Desire is a part of the creative and expansive process of the Universe.

There is a reason you chose to experience life on a physical platform, and that is so you can experience physically based perspectives. When you came into this life you agreed to forget what had gone before so you could focus on this life experience.

You are living a physical life from a physical perspective as a spiritual being flowing spiritual energy.

There are some that believe that having material desires are from a place of ego. If everything is energy and vibration on a deeper level, how can there be any difference between material desires and anything else? And remember that *your* desires are sovereign – what YOU want is important. If everyone had the same desires, the Universe would be a very 'similar' place.

The Universe is not a place of constraint and limitation, it is a place of freedom, abundance, choice and expression. You express yourself through the life that you live.

Remember, the Universe wants you to expand and grow, as it grows through you. You are an aspect and expression of the Universe and its desires. Desires are part of the creation process and taking them away is a way of not enabling your free flowing abilities as a natural creator. Instead, let your desires flow and align your beliefs and thoughts to your creations. *Let the universal energy flow through you and with you; be in synch with the rest of the Universe and see manifestations that you wouldn't believe.*

The reason most people do not get the manifestations they are desiring is because they are 'thinking' their manifestations rather than feeling and 'being'. When you are doing the latter, you are letting the Universe flow through you and letting it express itself.

When people 'think' their goals rather than 'be' them, it is usually because somewhere their conscious 'thinking' mind is involved. Whether it be about the attainment of the goal and what it means for them or the 'how' in the acquisition of it, or any associations about it altogether. *The way you know is by how it feels.*

Are you 'thinking' about what you want and not feeling many emotions, or do you easily step into the joy and delight of it as you think about it? *You want your goals to evoke emotions in you* – that is an indicator of them activating your vibration about them. If they do not stir you, they are likely to be from a thinking, analytical, rational place, and that does not stir the workings of the Universe in the same way as through your vibration.

As an example, if you are wanting a lover but he or she has to be someone that will love you unconditionally. If you explore *why* you have the requirement that he or she loves you unconditionally and it turns out that the motivation is so that you do not get hurt, then part of your motivation is fear based. It is likely that the goal will not feel so good and it will be more from a 'thinking' place of "*I would like a lover*" rather than an experiential place of you imagining what it would be like to be with someone that moves you deeply in the most delightful of ways.

What is more important than the words that you use to describe what you want is the vibration and emotion about what you are wanting. The words you use will influence how you feel about it, but remember *the key thing is how you feel about it.*

If you are wanting someone to love you unconditionally because *"She (or he) makes my heart sing and the unconditional love we express is so beautiful,"* that sounds like a more positive vibration than *"I want her (or him) to love me unconditionally so that she (/ he) doesn't hurt me some day."*

The key is not in the words but in the feelings and vibration in them and behind them. You attract through your vibration.

Something to also remember is that when you have evaluations and judgements about other's goals, when you make a judgement and have negative emotion about it, you are taking *yourself* out of your own flow, regardless of *their* goals.

Others are free to have the desires they choose as part of their evolution, as are you.

Your joy and 'journey' is to have your thoughts and beliefs become very familiar about you and your desires being together. Practice having them in your mind. Build the vibrational familiarity. **Your world and your reality are composed of vibration. When you change your vibration, you change your reality, and your world.**

You came to your physical life with the intention of living it from a physical perspective. You chose to forget who you are –

your larger non-physical self - momentarily, so that you could focus on this physical life and create in it and experience it.

To let what you want into your experience, you need to be a vibrational match to it. You cannot want something but be vibrating about something else. It is like wanting to listen to a certain radio station but tuning into another – you have to *be vibrationally receptive to what you want by having your thoughts and feelings from it.* If you are thinking thoughts – and more significantly, feeling emotions - and emitting a different vibration, you will be attracting different outcomes.

Your 'Problems' Truly Are How You See Them

'Problems' are what they are because of the perception you have about them. You know very well that as your perception has changed about a situation in the past, it has changed from being a problem to being something else. Oftentimes even an opportunity or a blessing.

What keeps something as a 'problem' is exactly that – the perception that it is a problem. That label creates a boundary around it. Add to that the emotions that you have about it being a problem and anger, resentment, feelings of regret, guilt, fear, and anything else, that binds it as a problem even more. *You can see emotions as the vibrational 'glue' that bind your reality.* When you have emotions about something, they further cement it to your reality by what you believe about it – whether for the better or for the worse.

The reason you see something as a problem is because of the beliefs you have about it. You may perceive certain eventualities or consequences which you do not want to experience and as a result you see this situation as a problem. You see it not

65

working out satisfactorily, and you see the consequences and voila! You have a 'problem'.

Seeing something as a problem is a process that you do internally to keep seeing it that way. You also have processes for experiencing joy, delight, love, passion, and more. Are you aware of the thoughts you are thinking and the processes you are running internally to experience these states?

When it comes to a problem, make peace with the consequences. Be at peace with it no matter how you see it turning out. Take the pressure away from it. **When you are at peace with all scenarios, you are then living in your now and not biased by potential perceived eventualities, and the fear of what may or may not happen.** When you are truly in that place of peace, the Universe will have been hearing and 'feeling' that vibration and you are more likely to experience scenarios in accordance with that 'peace'.

Also, when you are at peace and there is less 'noise' in the way of fear and other 'distracting' emotions, you are offering the vibration of what you want VERY cleanly and purely (without contradiction). You do not need to be loud for the Universe to hear you. But if you are clear and congruent, the Universe will more easily hear you.

The situations you experience in your life offer variety and diversity. You can see them as sticking points, or as the tapestry you experience in your life. *It is up to you which perspectives you choose for yourself, and that will determine how you feel about them, how you respond to them, and what resources – within you and outside you – will be drawn to you.*

Know that no matter what the situation, you were not sent without the resources for handling it. When you also realise that your existence is beyond this physical life, it also takes a lot of pressure off it. Make the most of this life and your moments, and know that you are adored by the Universe.

When you label something as a problem, that is the vibration that you are offering about it. You attract more of the same vibration.

It is not easy for the Universe to give you blue when you have painted your picture in red and you keep saying: "Don't give me red! Don't give me red!" What is your attention on?

On a deeper level, the Universe does not judge or make evaluations. You do on a physical level. You are what puts labels on what 'things' are. All possibilities are always open. And the Universe has unconditional love for everything. *It is your choice how you want to perceive things, and consequently how you want to let them affect you.*

When something happens that you are not happy about, use it to *focus on what you DO want.* It is easy to get pulled into things and our attention to grow and grow on those things. Instead, say to yourself "I don't want this, but I want this instead, and I want this, and this, and this. And I'm going to like this about this and won't this be wonderful? And also this and in this colour in this shape and size and...." and *immerse yourself in the vibration of what you want, not on what you don't want.*

67

*Take your attention off the problem, and put it on the
solution. You may not even know the solution, but start to
notice how it feels to have it, and build the vibration
from there.*

It is easy to get pulled into the emotions of a problem and make
evaluations about ourselves and our lives. Instead, turn it to
how you want things to be, and make evaluations about that.
Think about your life and you in respect to it. Build and
practice that vibration so that it's the most familiar to you.

*You are planting in a fertile ground with the vibration that
you offer. You choose the emotions and thoughts that you
have and influence what grows in this garden that
is your reality.*

Your 'problems' are scenery that you are passing and labelling
them as you are. When you change how you label them and
how they affect you, how you and the Universe responds to
them, changes.

From Every Experience You Have,
You Have a New Platform

*Everything that you experience in your life serves as a
platform. You came here to LIVE life and EXPERIENCE
it. You didn't come to sit on the sidelines and observe it.*

Through your experience of something, it creates changes within
you. Whether it is on a neurological level – if you want to

consider it from a scientific or medical perspective, or a vibrational level – if you want to consider it from a spiritual or metaphysical perspective. You are expanding vibrationally in every moment. Whether it be through deliberate intent, or through the observations that you make. *In your constant growing, your perspectives are evolving and expanding, as are your insights.*

You never look back on the same thing with the same eyes. You always look back on it with new eyes and new perspectives, even on a subtle level. You can never truly make the same mistakes again because things will always be different on a deeper level.

Each 'mistake' (and again, that is a perspective - it does not need to be seen as a 'mistake'), will be a new experience. Eventually, you may make other choices and go down different paths, but those successive outcomes served towards your clarity, and far more than any intellectual insights that you gained. They served your clarity on a vibrational level.

Everything you experience is creating a vibrational platform. Each platform has insights and perspectives you did not have previously. You can never look back with the same eyes, but with the vibrational experience and clarity that you have gained along your way.

You may have always wanted to be a millionaire in your life. When you become a millionaire, you see the world from different eyes (just as you would have throughout the journey also). You may then decide that you want to have another home to live in, or that you would like a yacht. This viewpoint wasn't available to you from your previous perspectives because of the beliefs that you had then, but it is available to you now because of the viewpoint that you have currently.

69

It is important to remember that it is not because of what is or is not in your life that you have the viewpoints that you do, it is always to do with *your* perceptions, which is based on your beliefs, emotions, observations etc.

THE RELATIONSHIP BETWEEN THE WORLD THAT YOU SEE, AND THE WORLD THAT YOU FEEL

The Physical and the Non-Physical Worlds are Both Aspects of Your Reality

Have you noticed that when you use a magnifying glass and focus in on something it is so much sharper and clearer and you have a deeper experience of it? That is what the physical dimension you are in provides.

This physical playground creates a context for you to expand and grow. To make decisions and choices and see the physical manifestations. To experience the variety and contrast and desires and have new intentions of which to have further manifestations.

Your physical world provides a rich, full, and vivid experience. It is being in the driving seat of the car and having an experience of being in it, whereas the non-physical experience would be from another perspective. That is what you came into your physical life for, to have this life experience and for the Universe to experience itself through *your* perspective. *You, just like everything else there is, are an important – and unique – aspect for the Universe to experience itself through your eyes.*

If the Universe was only 'one', there would be no way it could see itself and experience itself. Hence, everything around you is an aspect of the Universe – and of the Universe – experiencing itself.

71

It can be said that your physical life is like a dream that you are living. The spiritual aspect of you has come into this life to have experiences that you do and it is like a dream. When you return to non-physical you wake up and remember who you are. But when living the physical life, many forget that they are something much broader than their physical life and body. They are spirit manifest in physical form to experience life and to flow energy through your desires.

You didn't come to this life to be small. You came to ask for your heart's desires and in your clear calling the Universe would bring the resources and manifestations to fit. And in doing so, you and the Universe would both expand and grow, and want more. It is about the living and the flowing of energy for your desires than in the acquisition and 'having' of them.

The physical world is very different to the non-physical. Both are different vibrations and different densities. The physical world is sharper and focused, energetically, and provides vivid experiences. The non-physical is softer and lighter with less density.

Due to the sharpness and intensity of the physical environment, the emotions and sensations are more pronounced there. Much like a rollercoaster, the ride you have on the physical plane is more thrilling, that's why you chose it so.

In thinking of your desires you are channelling universal energy through you by your attention to them. Them feeling good is an indication of the energy that you are flowing through you. This universal energy can be thought of as Source energy, God energy, Life force, or anything else, even God flowing through you.

72

You are living in a Universe which is not just physical but also non-physical and spiritual in nature. They are not separate worlds but are one, existing together at different frequencies. *This is very much why it is a world where what you see is based on what frequency, or vibration, that you are offering.*

The world has a myriad of possibilities, and will give you what you are choosing to see, through your vibration.

You are the physical manifestation of your essence. It is the same with everything else around you. *There is a vibrational and non-physical, or energetic, reason for everything that is around you.* There is no 'coincidence'.

You Have Possibilities Beyond What You See

You have been used to living a life where the possibilities that you see are based on what you have already seen. You have been used to looking at what is around you to determine what is possible, and what is not.

The drawback with that is that you can only expand and grow based on your observations of what has already gone before. You would not allow yourself to think of possibilities beyond them if you are focusing only on them and attracting more of the same.

For example, if you have been used to having a moderate income and that is the way you feel about it, you will be offering a similar vibration to attract more of the same. You are looking at what has happened so far, rather than using your imagination and *envisioning* how you want things to be.

73

If you are only looking at what has gone before - whether in your own life or in other's lives - you are limiting yourself to the potential available to you.

If you have had a moderate income, how about exploring what a great income would be like? Can you imagine that experience for yourself? Can you get magazines or books or watch programmes where you can experience this? Do you know someone (or someone who knows someone) who is living a life like that, that you can meet or be around and experience what this would be like? You don't have to necessarily agree with everything about them, you are just wanting to evoke the vibration of what you do want, and resonate with, within you.

What if all possibilities have always been open to you and all you had to do was adjust your vibration to harmonise with the possibilities for them to enter your life?

You do not necessarily have to have others around you that have already acquired what you are wanting. You can use your imagination and practice in your mind how it would feel. What would it be like? What would you think and feel, and how would you be? These may be possibilities not even considered before when one assumes the status quo of what is already around them.

When one never looks above the imaginary ceiling – or assumes that there is nothing beyond the ceiling - they are blind to possibilities that they do not know exist.

We make no judgement on what possibilities one should look at or not look at. That is a personal decision based on what one resonates with and where they are in their own evolution.

The point we are making is oftentimes people are very used to assuming that life is a certain way because of past patterning and conditioning. Allow yourself to put that aside, put any presumptions and beliefs aside, and ask yourself what you would like to experience more of in your life.

You do not need to know 'how' to have it; you just need to be offering a vibration and feeling of it. If you congruently do that, without doubting it, it will attract more thoughts and experiences of the same and the momentum will build and build.

All possibilities have always been open to you. You have always had the 'magic lamp' in your lap. If you have only been asking for miniscule things based on your attention to them, then that is what you have been getting more of. This is a vibrational Universe where there is no separation between you and anything else. You are always connected, other than through the separation you believe from your perspectives about it.

The Universe will give you whatever you ask for. Your power is in your asking and alignment to it with your thoughts. If your attention is on the challenges that you have had then that is what your vibrational tone will be and what you are 'asking', and that is what the Universe will hear and give you more of.

Focus on the thought and vibration of what you want and the Universe will orchestrate chance after chance after chance. Thought is vibration, and vibration attracts more of the same. You attract manifestations that are a corresponding vibration to what you have been giving off

Limitation, scarcity, and competition, are concepts based on fear and lack - not abundance, prosperity and possibility. When you THRIVE and see the possibilities, it won't matter what others do, you will be too much in your own flow and seeing and finding all you need to have whatever you want

Every Moment is a Fresh Canvas Where All Possibilities Exist

The Universe is a blank canvas where all possibilities exist. You are an expression of it here in the physical. What would you like to paint upon this possibility that you call your 'life'? What would you like to experience in it?

Your every now moment has fresh possibilities. It is a fertile ground where you can plant anything you like upon it. You have freewill in this Universe because you can think any thought you like. And because you can think any thought you like, you can offer any vibration you like.

What happens is people bias their now with what they bring across from the past. That is fine, but the thing to ask yourself is does it serve you, or limit you.

76

We all have habitual patterns of thought. Behaviourally we have them so as to make our lives easier. It is easier for our unconscious minds to regulate our blood pressure, digestive system, breathing, and deal with things automatically so that we do not have to think about everything on a conscious level.

We generalise behaviours and thoughts so as to make life easier and more efficient. If we were consciously dealing with all the details in each moment, we may not have the space to do other things.

The issue that occurs is when we generalise things which do not serve us. So if we have experiences with negative emotions and we associate the negative emotion to that experience or person or place for *every* single occurrence, then we disempower ourselves.

So the next time we see that person or are in a similar place, we feel things which do not help us. And of course, if we are offering a vibration of something we dislike, we are keeping ourselves in that place, vibrationally. If we are busy focusing on something that we dislike, we are not instead focusing on something that we may be wanting and letting that come into our lives.

When someone goes into fresh new moments in their lives with habits of thought, they 'fill' the potential possibilities in that now moment, and do not utilise the potential of – and 'live' - each moment. Their attention is on the patterned behaviour than responding in the now.

With the same habits of thoughts, people find themselves creating the same situations in their lives - commensurate with the same thoughts they have been having. It may not necessarily be the exact same people and places necessarily, although it may, it would be scenarios which are a match to the vibration they are offering. The details may appear different, but they would still be a match to the vibration the individual was offering with their thoughts.

They might find themselves leaving their job or leaving a love...and then going into another job or another relationship with similar or same dynamics. What has happened is whilst they have changed their environment and what is on the outside, they have not changed their vibration and what they are asking of the Universe. The actors may have changed but the script hasn't, so to speak.

The Universe is malleable with your thought. It responds to you. It is in a dance with you, and the music is vibration.

We Have Been Used to Playing, Dreaming and Creating Wonderful Lives

As children, we used to dream and allow ourselves to think of what we would LOVE. As we grew older, we took on beliefs that would constrict us in our thinking and allowing of possibilities. We took on responsibilities in life – and in our minds - and equated them to mean less options and possibilities.

It's like growing older and assuming that every decade you will have one less limb that you can use. If you believed that, your body may have the limb, but due to your belief about it, you would not be harnessing its capabilities.

Realise, you are not just a physical being. *No matter what is happening in your life on a physical level and who is in it, it does not change the fact that you have all the resources of the Universe at your disposal.* Through your thoughts and non-physical energy, you have access to that.

But because of who is in their lives or what is happening, many get focused on the day to day issues and you are so absorbed by them, they do not see the full capabilities they have. Step back. *Look at the broader perspective.* Your life as a whole. You are a spiritual being who is eternal beyond this physical shell and who will have endless opportunities to live, experience, create, and grow.

The truth is you can never truly constrict your options other than through the beliefs you have about yourself and your life.

You can paint with black and white, or you can use a whole spectrum of colours and bring to life what is in your heart.

What you experience in life is a REFLECTION of your thoughts.

The Universe Has Infinite Possibilities

The Universe is prosperous and abundant beyond what you can ever imagine. The physical world may appear discrete and quantifiable, the non-physical world is more abstract and unquantifiable.

If you realise that in every moment, every thought that you are having is expanding the Universe, can you imagine how much it is expanding with the thoughts that are being thought of as a collective whole?

79

The Universe has infinite possibilities. What are you creating with yours? As children, we would be used to exploring boundless possibilities, and playing for the fun of it. We would enjoy playing and creating in this playground we are in. And in offering that vibration, we would be calling forth those things which are commensurate with the joyful environment there is.

Despite how the world may have appeared to you for many years, **when you find the joy within you, the world you see changes. When you change the eyes that you look at the world with, the world you see reflects that.**

If your life is a blank canvas where all possibilities truly exist, what would you like to see in it?

The Universe Accepts You Totally

The whole Universe is malleable matter on a deeper level. It is wellbeing and 'goodness', and inherently positive. How can it be anything else other than what you are on a deeper level? You are of the same substance.

The Universe is positive wellbeing, and when it does not appear that way, it is because you are not letting in the light by blocking it with your beliefs and thoughts.

The word 'love' is often romanticised, but if you imagine you – and the Universe – on a non-physical level are unconditionally accepting, 'love' becomes a very understandable and natural word. Source energy, the non-physical equivalent and all-that-is, is pure love. It does not judge, it just 'is'. Love is the norm.

It's from a physical perspective that evaluations and judgements and acceptance come in. ***On a non-physical level there isn't a need for acceptance, because it just is; it's assumed.*** The separation, or the notion of separation, comes from a physical perspective.

You are actually 'one' and connected to everything else. But from the physical perspective that you have, you see separation. The reason you are 'separate' from everything else, is that you are an aspect of the Universe and in your separateness the Universe can 'see' itself and experience itself. If the Universe was just 'one', it couldn't see and experience itself. But through all the aspects of it, it can experience itself. And each aspect is just as much of the Universe as the other.

When you are closer to the vibration of love and appreciation, you are closer to non-physical 'you' who you really are on a deeper level. As you are closer and closer to that place, you will see the synchronicities and manifestations in your life more and more because ***you will be closer to your own natural flow.***

<u>You are Connected to Everything that Exists</u>

On a deeper level, there is no space and time. Space and time are physical constructs rather than them existing on a non-physical or spiritual level. We constructed them to experience life on a physical plane and to have the contrast and experiences that we do. They add the sharpness and focus to this physical dimension.

Then, from our manifestations, we would have more desires and wants from the new perspectives we would have, and manifest those. From there we would have further desires and preferences, and so on. It is an eternal and infinite expansion.

All the time, you and the Universe expand beautifully, in concert, together.

On a deeper level you are interacting with your environment in a beautiful dance and synchronisation. You are in total harmony with all around you even though it may not always seem like it. *There is a parallel between what is outside of you and what is within you.*

The objects of the world are permanent as long as you focus on them; put your attention on something else and that becomes 'permanent'.

The truth of the matter is *you are connected to everything that exists*. There is no separation. You are individual and unique and you are getting to live out the desires that are in *your* heart (which also happen to be the Universe's desires also - you are an extension of the Universe, after all!).

You are at choice and freewill to live out your desires and have them as what you want. The Universe will send matches of your vibration for you to co-create with.

You Experience That Which You Most Believe to Be

On a deeper spiritual level, *all possibilities exist in an unmanifest, pure potential form*. On a physical level, we experience the manifestations of those things that we most believe to see in our experience. We 'allow in', from the non-physical, that which we expect to be. We may not always be conscious of these beliefs, but the Universe works on this without fail, every time.

82

On a spiritual level there is no time or space - they are aspects of the physical world and help create contrast and desire. In essence, everything that you want is here and now. It is a matter of lining up to it and letting it manifest into to your physical experience.

When you only look at the physical form around you, you are not used to taking into account the unseen that is around you, and which is so much more.

When you *only* take physical actions to have what you want, without the energetic alignment, you are making it so much harder and longer a process (if you do not have the alignment) for yourself than would otherwise be the case. Alignment is when you are thinking and feeling from having your outcome. *It is those thoughts that naturally excite you about it.* They will lead to further thoughts that excite you, and so on.

The Universe is pure potential infinite. All possibilities exist. There is nothing that is not possible. The only 'limitations' are what you believe and let into your reality.

If you see the world around you as vibration – energy vibrating at a minute level so rapidly that it forms physical 'matter', and your thoughts also as vibration, and like vibrations attract, *you can see how fluid this world is.*

As you read these words, notice how they feel to you. *If they uplift you, they are resonating with you and communicating to who you are on a deeper level.* There is no coincidence you have this book in your hand. It is a vibrational match to your beliefs; and a confirmation. It is reminding you of who you are.

The Universe loves you unconditionally. It never withdraws anything from you. It is whether YOU 'let it in'.

83

You could say the Universe is light, and it is about how much of it you are letting in. Any darkness we experience is as a result of us resisting the wellbeing. There is no darkness, but more so an absence of light.

Your natural state is of love, joy, and feeling good. That is what you came here for - to line up your energy and create wonderful manifestations. From those new vantage points and perspectives created, you would have new desires and create more, and so on - *a continual and eternal expansion and growth.*

There is no ending; the Universe is eternal and infinite. And so are you - you are much more than your physical body.

All possibilities exist around you all the time. What you want already exists and it is about you tuning in to it by your attention to it.

It starts as a dream. Add helpings of faith and bake in an oven of expectation, and you soon have a reality

You Can Guide Others To Their Light, It Is Their Choice to See It

There is only goodness, wellbeing, and positivity. Anything otherwise is due to an absence and blocking of it. You may ask about conditions that you see in the world and how they can exist. They exist because they are matches to that experience. If you want to support them to wellbeing, do not see them from a place of lack, but see them how you wish them to be. Feel the feelings of them having what they want.

You cannot 'make' someone have something, it is down to their vibrational alignment. You can be a wonderful inspiration for them. In your connection to who you are, you can inspire someone else to theirs. This is VERY attractive.

You cannot help someone who is poor by you being poor. *But through your vibration and knowingness of the abundance there is, you can be a perfect vibrational example for them. You can reveal the light to them, it is up to them to see it.* It does not even need to be by you doing or saying anything. They will feel it and know it. It will be up to them whether it is something for them to move towards and follow the light that you are offering. That is their choice. Just as you have freewill and choice, so do they.

You may want something for someone else, but if you deny them the right to make the choices that they are free to make and came here as a creator to make, they will feel it, and it won't feel comfortable. The key is whether you are bringing them closer to the connection of who they are - towards their flow - or not. That will determine how helpful it is for them and how they will feel about it.

When you uplift someone and raise their vibration, they feel good and will be drawn to you – they are being drawn by their connection of who they are. When what you are offering is constricting and limiting, they will feel uncomfortable and be drawn away.

You can be a wonderful inspirer by seeing them as the physical and the non-physical being that they are and realising how it is perfect for them to be who they are, where they are, and how they are.

85

They may not like where they are at, in their lives. Though by you being aware of vibration and the things that they do not see – such as all that they want already being in vibration, you can help them be at peace with it and soothe that vibration.

From that place, you can help them to orient towards where they *do* want to be. *Again, your faith and knowingness is the greatest light you can offer them. It is their choice whether in that moment they want to be illuminated, or look towards the corner where there isn't light.*

There Is No Other Like You

From your perspective, you literally ARE the centre of the Universe, the heartbeat of it. There is no perspective the Universe can have like yours, which is why you are sovereign and valued. *There can be no other like you in the Universe, and who can offer what you do.*

There is no coincidence that you are here and have the thoughts that you do - you are meant to be here to provide your unique and valued perspective. *You are here to experience life from your perspective, and with the choices and viewpoints that you experience.*

Your viewpoint really IS the centre of the Universe as far as you are concerned. You can only see the world through your eyes.

You may feel empathy for another, but it is through *your* perspective. You can never truly and exclusively do something 'only' for another because you can never lose your own perspective; that will always be there. When you are doing something for someone else, you are doing it from your own perspective also because you cannot separate or remove it from the choices you make in your physical life.

This does not in any way lessen something you do for another. Not at all! The only distinction we are making is that no matter what you do for another, it can never be said that you are 'only' doing it for someone else, as that choice will be from your perspective and never truly 'selfless'. There is nothing wrong with that. You came to live life from your perspective and do things for others and for yourself from *that* perspective.

There is also no judgement in your choices. You are a free being. The Universe thrives and revels in your choices, and expansion, as thus it expands too. It is from you living from *your* perspective that the Universe wants you to be.

There will be no other, ever, that will paint the Universe the way that you do. You were born to paint it with your colours and your style. No one will ever leave a footprint on the Universe like yours.

The World Does Not Need 'Fixing'

The Universe is perfect; it does not need fixing nor is it 'broken'. One just needs to make peace with their perspective and they will see this reflected more and more in their reality. *They will see back reflected whatever perspective they have. That is all you will ever get – a reflection back of your beliefs.*

You may see things in your physical reality which disturb you and alarm you and you may feel compassion for others and perhaps even an injustice for the way things are. On a vibrational level, there are no coincidences.

87

The situations of lack and despair have vibrational undercurrents which have led to those situations - it's a physical world within a vibrational Universe. On some level, there is also a vibration within you that has led to you observing them. Your world is totally dictated by your beliefs and perceptions – your vibration.

Change your beliefs, and the world you live in changes.

There may be tragedies in the world and you may feel compassion for people involved in them. See them as the light that they are and project that to them. *The way to help them is to see them as the solution, and not hold them in their despair by your attention to it.*

Empathising and caring for someone is absolutely fine. But do not keep yourself in the state where you are focusing on their pain and on what is wrong. That is not the vibration of the solution. *See the solution in their vibration.* They already have it in their vibration. It just hasn't manifested yet. See the solution that they do not yet see for themselves. And through your vision and inspiration for them – even without saying it – they will feel it and they will have a choice to follow the light, or focus on their despair.

If we cannot see a solution for another, at least take your attention away from what is wrong. Focus on other aspects of them which are not as emotionally loaded. If, for example, we cannot take our attention away from the poverty of a man, put it upon his smile or the fact that he cares for others or that he is a wonderful story teller.

By your appreciation of this, you are shining universal source energy at him which connects him to who he is and from where all his resources are. This is very different to seeing him as a

88

poor man and having a better intention for him. Notice the difference in how these feel, and use that as your guide.

Often people will say that the world can be a better place. This is implying that there is something 'wrong' with it. Whilst you may look around and see all sorts of things which displease you - such as famine, culture, wars, illnesses and much more - know that the Universe is in 'balance'. How could it be any other way? *What you see is a creation and an attraction from your own filters – this is the case with your entire physical experience.*

That does not mean it doesn't exist, but that everything you experience in your life is a manifestation of your beliefs and vibration.

The Universe is total, complete, infinite, abundant, and in balance. You will see the aspects of it that are in resonance with your vibration.

If you only see certain things in your reality and experience, it is more an indication of *your* vibration rather than the state of the Universe or planet.

Perception is projection.

The Universe is a playground for you to create in. If you want to focus on and see misery, you will see more of that. If you want to focus on and see sadness, you will see more of that. If you want to focus on and see more love, you will see more of that. If you want to focus on and see more joy, you will see more of that.

There is a vibrational reason behind everything. The physical world is a manifestation of vibration. If the vibrational causes are not addressed, the symptoms can manifest somewhere else. This is the same for the physical body as it is for the physical world.

You Inspire Others From Your Own Inspiration and Example

As you shine your light brighter you enable others to light their candles too.

Oftentimes people are concerned about following their joy because they feel they are being 'selfish'. The answer to this is that *in you being aligned to who you truly are on a deeper level and being in your flow and the magic and miracles that the Universe offers, you are inspiring others to do the same for themselves.* You are BEING the example for them. *That is the most useful thing that you can offer them - their own alignment to the prosperity that there is for them.*

In you being in your flow you are an inspiration to others.

You cannot create in someone else's reality but through your inspiration you inspire others to theirs and for them to create the magic and miracles that you will create in yours.

You can never be poor enough yourself to help someone in poverty. You can never be sick enough yourself to help someone who is sick. But through your alignment to abundance and wellbeing and the natural flow of the Universe that exists everywhere for everyone, you inspire others to theirs.

People won't need to hear this from you but *they will feel it.* Remember *there is FAR more that happens on an unseen level* than what you can see, although you can feel what is happening. Others will feel what is happening with you and it will resonate with them on a deeper level and encourage and guide and inspire them to their own alignment.

Your job here is to be you and the best you that you can be - *You Are Perfect Being You.*

THE STRUCTURE OF THE UNIVERSE THAT YOU LIVE IN

You Are Interconnected To Everything Else That Exists

People often go through life with a sense of separation and disconnection and loneliness. You can never be truly alone. The loneliness is an illusion. It is a perspective from your physical world. Yet you are interconnected to everything else and there is no separation. **When the rest of the Universe is talking to you in every moment, how can you ever be truly alone?** Only when you focus on what is not around you on the physical, and have unpleasant feelings about it.

In your recognition of your connection to everything else and your flow, you are attractive to everything else in the Universe. Your connection is very attractive, and attracts more of the same.

Remember, what you see around you is not all there is. It is just the tip of the iceberg. **The vast majority of what exists is non-physical and unseen, but felt and known through your emotions.** In the analogy of the iceberg, it is the dominant majority that is underneath the water. It is the source of everything that is physical.

Many people get frustrated because they cannot 'see' why things do not work. The reason is they are trying to solve things rationally or only by what they can see – the physical. And not everything will always have a clear physically observed answer.

93

Though it will always have an underlying non-physical vibrational cause.

The unseen is as part of nature and the natural world as what you see in nature in the physical world. It is just something that most people are not as familiar with, but it is at least as prevalent as anything you see in the physical world.

You see the greenery, the streams, the mountains and valleys. The unseen nature around you is as dominant a part of your reality as much as everything else is.

Man has not been used to believing things that cannot be seen. Now there is more and more of a realisation that there is more in our reality than can be seen. Also what is furthering that belief is that technology has been getting better and better and better able to detect these aspects of our reality. Things can be measured now that couldn't even be conceived before. Imagine what else will be appearing in its own time...

When it comes to your life, it is not just the physical body that you can see that is important. This physical body is a manifestation of 'You' - your joyful spirit - of so much more than you can see. This physical body is a manifestation of you as the eternal, divine, loving, wonderful spirit that you are. You have come to this physical playground to create and experience life on this plane. This life is a match to what you have been asking for on a vibrational level. You wouldn't be here otherwise. What you make of it now, is your choice.

The Connection With Manifesting & Law of Attraction

There are many that learn Law of Attraction and are only aware of the physical world. They are not aware of vibration nor of non-physical. They visualise what they want and take actions. But oftentimes for them it still 'doesn't work'. And in some cases they decide that Law of Attraction doesn't work or that it "doesn't work for everybody."

They feel that they have followed the formula that they have read in a book somewhere or somewhere else and it just hasn't happened for them. If someone is only following things from a physical perspective, at times they are likely to manifest and attract things, and if at other times they do not, by not being aware of the broader perspective – of vibration, they do not know what to adjust within themselves.

It's not about any technique or anything else. It's about what changes it makes within you and your vibration. That's what it's all about.

When people learn affirmations or visualise their goals or use other techniques, the key is really that they are using these techniques to adjust their vibration. *It is not about the techniques in and of themselves. It is what the techniques lead to in terms of the changes within themselves.* This is also why different people like different techniques – it is about the changes the techniques create within *them*.

When I have been teaching Law of Attraction to people all around the world, my intention is for them to be aware of vibration and non-physical and the full perspective about the Universe that they are in. When they are aware of this and they are trying to attract things or be in their flow, they have a greater understanding of what to adjust within themselves to make changes around themselves.

Now that you are aware of vibration and non-physical, you understand Law of Attraction, and the Universe around you, from a far broader perspective. You are getting a greater awareness of the world around you.

What's So Wonderful About This Universe?

This Universe is a wonderful place to be existing in. *It gives you total freewill to choose your perspective and experience the reality that is a match to it, vibrationally.*

You can be suspicious about the world or negative about it, or be aware of your wellbeing and be allowing it. *The Universe, or world, will reinforce whatever beliefs that you have about it.*

You have total choice and freewill. Many are not aware of this and they have limiting beliefs about what they can have or be or do. They believe that because they were born in a certain location or family or social status, that it can inhibit or limit what is possible for them.

Notice structurally what this does. When someone believes that they are inhibited, it prevents them from activating the beliefs - and vibration - of the things that they want. So the location or family or social status or anything else may not be preventing them, but the individual's belief that it limits them *prevents them from activating the thoughts to actually attract what they want.*

This is why I will often say to people that they should allow themselves to dream and practice the thoughts of what they would like. Allow themselves to fantasise. "If you could, what would it be like?" Allow themselves to play out the scenario of "*What if...?*" What if it could happen, what would it be like? What if you *could* have what you want? What if...?

"What if...?"

Many people are too easily sold on their limitations rather than being open-minded on their possibilities. In fact, they *assume* their limitations, which is even more dangerous because it is not a conscious awareness. They just implicitly accept them. **They do not allow themselves to look beyond what they see and realise that there is a whole world out there.**

"If you could, what would it be like?"

They do not allow themselves to offer a vibration of what they want. They just need to start doing that and not doubt or contradict it. **When they start to imagine it and it feels good, the Universe is already working in their favour. They just need to carry on along that stream and the Universe will provide them with more examples of how it IS possible.**

The Universe loves you so unconditionally that if you want to place conditions on yourself, it will even allow you to do that.

You are an aspect and an expression of the Universe and are it, and it is you. Just like drop in the ocean, you are a part of it, and individual too. The Universe gets to experience itself through your perspective, as it does through all other aspects of itself.

You can never be separate from the Universe, you can never be disconnected. You are always a part of the whole. A unique, very valued, and special part.

Qualities of The Universe

Inherent within the Universe are certain qualities. These are prevalent in everything and everywhere - in All-That-Is.

The Universe is intelligence and it is free flowing. It has a connectedness and information flows freely throughout it. When there is resistance or a lessening of communication, there can be a disconnection from the well-being of the Universe. This is the same in physical bodies as it is in other entities within the Universe.

The Universe is abundant and infinite. If it is abundant and infinite and there is intelligence and it is free flowing, this abundance and infiniteness is available to all within the Universe.

There is pure potential. The Universe is a fertile ground for your creation. The Universe responds and reflects your vibration. It acts like an echo.

There is nothing that does not exist. Everything is existing now. If something does not exist, it will not be existing now. *Energy does not die. It is transferred and changes form.*

In every part, there is the whole. The Universe is holographic in nature. There is interconnectedness and information sharing between everything.

The Universe is always expanding, it cannot not. It is paradoxical in that energy does not die and is not created, but the Universe expands within itself as it does.

The Universe is always fluid and expansive and expanding. Nothing is ever fixed. Everything is vibrating and recreating. Everything you experience – including you and your body, are always recreating in each moment.

You only experience the same things – such as bodily conditions, experiences in your life etc – because you are recreating them with the same thought, or more precisely, the same vibrational patterns.

All possibilities exist. If everything is thought and everything is vibration, one eventuality is just like another. The Universe doesn't differentiate. You do, through your perceptions and beliefs.

What you see is only the manifestation of what you have believed so far. There is so much more than that. What would you like to allow into your life next...

VIBRATION: BRINGS YOU AND WHAT YOU WANT TOGETHER

Underlying everything that you see around you, and even that which you do not, there is a vibration. Everything is vibrating on a deeper level. In this Universe, like vibration attracts like vibration.

Everything Is Vibration; You Live In a Vibrational Universe

Everything is vibrating on a deeper level. What you see around you as matter appears that way because it is vibrating so quickly that it appears as solid. This is how we have different solids - because they are vibrating at different levels. The reason heat is what it is, is because it is vibrating at a faster rate than what cold is.

At a cinema, when a film projects onto the screen, it is (or used to be) at a rate of 24 frames per second; thus giving the impression of movement. This is the same with everything around you. It is vibrating on a deeper level and *vibrating so quickly that it appears as solid.* Over 80% of what you see around you is 'space'; it is because it is vibrating so quickly that it appears solid.

The reality that you experience around you is a reflection of your perspective. It may not necessarily always be your conscious or deliberate perspective; it is nevertheless *a reflection of you and the vibration that you are giving off.*

Nothing happens around you by chance or by coincidence. It is given invitation, so to speak, by your vibration.

Many people do not find it easy to change their perspective because they believe that "things are the way that they are" (this is a belief in itself). They are not necessarily even conscious of the concept of beliefs and perceptions.

It is easier to change your perspective than reality. Changing your perspective will change your reality.

The way that you see the world - every element of the way that you see the world - is a belief and a perspective. **And most importantly, and especially so, are the things that you assume about the world and the way that it is.** These are your most ingrained of beliefs. These are the beliefs that you are least conscious of because you assume them so easily and assume that the world is this way and that's it.

When you think of what you want, it is on its way. At that moment, you are emanating a vibration that is a match to it. It is a matter of are you allowing it (or are you resisting it).

In you raising your vibration and feeling good, the manifestations that you experience in your life will correspond with how you feel. **What you attract can only be within vibrational vicinity of what you are emitting. The better you feel, the better your manifestations.**

The Emotional Scale

If you consider an emotional scale, where lower down the scale you have emotions that do not feel very good, such as depression, anger etc, and as you progress further up the scale, the emotions feel better and better. Along the way there can be hope, and towards the top there can be joy, love, appreciation, and other emotions that feel delightful.

The emotions that you experience, are an indication of your alignment from 'you' (physical you) and 'You' (non-physical or spiritual you). The better you feel, the greater your alignment, and vice versa.

The worse the emotion feels, the greater the indication it is of your 'resistance' of who you are – of you allowing the non-physical aspect of you to flow through you physically. The better the emotion feels, the greater the indication it is of your 'allowing' of who you are. *The more you are allowing, the greater the flow of universal energy through you and the more in sync you are with everything around you.*

If we experience resistance and are blocking our flow, it can feel uncomfortable - at varying degrees, depending upon the resistance - and this can further increase and eventually lead to physiological symptoms, and more. The key is to be aware of the discomfort and resistance when it occurs, and identify how you are creating that negative emotion or perspective within you and shift it so that you are more.

Sometimes it is not about having to make major changes. *It can be just a subtle shift in perspective so that you are 'freer' and more allowing in your outlook.* It is about letting energy flow through you and you being a part of the Universe than you

103

trying to separate and control the part of the Universe that you are in.

The physical manifestations and happenings that you experience in your life will be commensurate with the emotions - which are an indication of your vibration - that you offer.

When we experience emotions such as fear and anger, you can very much feel in the sensations that they are blocking off your energy, rather than being free flowing like love, joy or appreciation. Recognise this 'blocking off' of energy and adjust your perspective to allow it to flow.

As mentioned earlier in this book, we have been very much used to thinking that our physical outlook on things is the only thing that exists. There is an energy in everything and in all things which is more powerful than the physical that you see. Your connection to that energy is through your flow and your allowing of your own energy. That is where your synchronicities, manifestations, and magic will come from.

The Better You Feel, The Better The Manifestations

As someone goes further up the emotional scale, their thinking is likely to be more and more abundant and full of possibilities and choices. As someone goes lower down the emotional scale, they will be more likely to see less possibilities and choices and be more 'fixed' in their perspectives.

'Need' and 'lack' and perspectives of scarcity are derivatives of emotions lower down the scale. Creativity, inspiration, synchronicity, and more, are derivatives of emotions further up the scale. *The manifestations that you experience from any of these emotions, will be a match to the vibration that you offer.*

Lower down the emotional scale there are denser emotions, whereas at higher vibrations things will be more fluid and fast flowing.

When you raise your vibration, you increase your possibilities and open yourself up to the possibilities from the Universe that are a match. You are more in alignment with your faster moving energetic current than when lower down the vibrational scale. *Your flow from the spiritual is infinite. It is about your allowing of it.*

Your Vibration and Law of Attraction

Everything in the Universe has a vibration, including your thoughts. Your thoughts - which influence your emotions - are the quickest way to change your vibration.

When you change your vibration, you attract thoughts that are more of a match to this new frequency. It is like a radio, in changing your vibration, you are adjusting your frequency and influencing what you experience in your life.

Law of Attraction is a law of the Universe. *Things within the Universe that are of a like vibration are drawn to each other.* When you change your vibration, you will attract things that are a match to this new vibration. It can start with ideas and inspiration, and as the momentum and mass builds - due to Law of Attraction - you attract more physical manifestations.

The thing that happens for many people is that they start to think about what they like but then they doubt or have fear and that contradicts the vibration they have been building.

The thing to do is to enjoy the process of thinking and feeling about what feels good. Do it for the joy of the process. Sometimes people do it for a result and then have negative associations about that result which compromise what they are trying to attract. *The key thing is to enjoy whatever it is you are focusing on.*

If you do something for the love of it, you can never lose.

Do you remember when you first fell in love? How did it feel? You had your attention on this all the time, didn't you? And it was because you LOVED doing so. It was a total joy, pleasure, and passion!

When you are trying to attract something and do not have much emotion about it, ask yourself why. Look into what your motivation is for having it. Is some of it 'need' based or focused on lack?

Find the joy in what you are trying to manifest or adjust what you are wanting so that it resonates deep within your soul. What you will also find is that by you adjusting your frequency to something you have a lot of positive feelings about, you will attract many other things along the way that match that also. *You will be attractive to so many things.*

106

Remember, it is not about the goal or 'thing' you are trying to attract but the energy that you flow through yourself. You are a spiritual being that flows energy through a physical body. The better you feel, the better you are doing that.

As you focus on something that you love, you will draw to yourself all sorts of things that are a match to it. It may start with ideas, it may be conversation with others. Perhaps you will catch something on television or an article somewhere, or it may be that someone approaches you who has something to do with what you have been focusing on. All in all, the momentum builds and you get to experience more of what you are focusing on. This is Law of Attraction.

"Pure" Vibration

A pure vibration is when your attention is on what you want and you are not contradicting it with thoughts and feelings to the contrary.

If you are thinking about attracting more money into your life, then a pure vibration would be for you to have your thoughts and feelings about what feels good about it, and not on what doesn't. It would, for example, be about focusing on what you would do with the money such as where you would go, what you would buy and whatever else you would do with the money that feels good.

If you were putting your attention on the lack of money or the challenges associated in acquiring the money or in worrying about what you would do with it, emotionally, these are very different to the joy of actually having it. You can *feel* the difference.

A pure vibration would be you focusing on what feels good. *The indication would be your emotions. When you focus purely on something, it feels good. The more purely, the better it feels.* The reason for this is you are channelling pure universal energy. You are not mixing the energy with resistant thoughts to the contrary.

When you are offering thoughts about what you want and what you do not want, you are sending a mixed vibration - mixed signals - to the Universe.

This is why people do not get what they are wanting. Because they are contradicting their vibration. Some people may visualise money but the next morning when they get a bill, they step into fear mode and emanate that vibration which contradicts all the other good work that they have done about having prosperity.

When you offer a pure vibration, the Universe sends a flood of resources to you in matching your vibration. It cannot resist you; if you are a vibrational match, you cannot not have the vibrational match to it.

Vibrational Matches, Conflicts, and Sabotaging Success

The reason that you and what you want are not together is because you have not been vibrational matches so far. This is like someone who wants to be in a relationship but all the time is talking about how relationships are so terrible and what can go wrong and why one should be afraid of them.

108

The pleasurable desire to be in a relationship and the fear of being in one are contradictory vibrations. You would be sending mixed signals to the Universe. So what would happen is either you would attract very little, or you would find yourself in relationships and sabotaging them.

When someone has desire and fear at the same time, they are likely to attract very little. This can be called a *simultaneous incongruity* because the motivation – pull (desire) and push (fear) are at the same time and are incongruous of each other.

When someone has desire and they attract what they want, and then the fear kicks in – because they now have what they want and the fear becomes very real – this can be called a *sequential incongruity*, because it occurs afterwards, in sequence. So someone acquires what they want, then fear or other contradictory emotions are activated – based on their emotional programming – and they sabotage their success. They either do things to damage what they have, or they give mixed signals which compromise what they have.

The Universe can only give you what you are a match to. If after having acquired something you are giving signals to the contrary of it, the Universe will match that. The key is to always focus on what feels best. That will orient you towards what is best for you in that moment.

Creating Deliberately

Everything in your experience in every moment is there because you are a match to it. This may not always necessarily always be conscious and deliberate.

109

Many people create in their lives by 'default' - by their 'pre-programming' and habits of thought they already have, rather than by deliberate intent. This is often unconscious rather than with conscious awareness.

This book is part of your journey in you becoming more conscious of what is happening around you and within you, and in you lining up and harmonising with all the possibilities that are available for you.

You could have the most wonderful magical lamp but not have the instructions. This book has been giving you instructions on so many levels. By your conscious awareness through the words that you read, your unconscious awareness by the patterns and beliefs that are implicit in the words, and on a vibrational level. *You drew this book to you before you were even aware of it. The book is a response to your asking. It has been clarifying your vibration about all of this in your life.*

What You Want Already Exists

Whenever you form a desire or a want or a preference, this has already manifested in vibration on a non-physical or spiritual level. You just haven't yet seen the manifestation of it in your physical world. In your attention or preference, *you have already created what you want.* The rest of the process is you being a vibrational match to it and it coming into your physical experience.

Your emotions indicate the alignment and congruency between you physically and you non-physically – the gap between 'you' and 'You'. When the gap and misalignment

110

increases, you will feel the discord through negative emotions. The negative emotions are an indicator of the widening gap.

As you close the gap between you physically and non-physically you feel better and better. There is exhilaration, excitement, joy, love, and many other positive emotions. The better it feels, the more aligned you are to who you truly are.

You may always have thought that your physical body was all that you were, but you are so much more than that. *Remember; you are an essence, an aspect of God, which has come into this physical body.* You are a drop in the beautiful ocean of the larger consciousness - but a significant and valued and loved and adored drop. A drop, whose preferences and desires are valued.

As you feel better and better you will know that you are getting more and more aligned with what you want and are a vibrational match. The more a vibrational match you are, the sooner you see it in your physical reality.

When you are a vibrational match to an essence or quality, you cannot have anything other than an expression of that essence or quality come into your life.

When you focus and feel from a place of having something, like love or prosperity or some other essence or quality, when you offer the vibration of it, the Universe will send experiences that are a match to that vibration.

111

It's About The Energy Behind Your Actions Than The Actions Themselves

Many people think that the way to become a match to what you want is by taking lots and lots of action. Action in itself is not vibration, although taking action is one way to influence vibration, and we will talk more about this in the next section. *Law of Attraction works on vibration – we live in a vibrational Universe.*

Many assume that taking lots and lots of action will lead to having what you want. *It is not actually the action that does it, but the refinement in vibration that leads to you having what you want, in this Universe that orchestrates vibrational matches.*

Some would say, "How can you have something without taking an action?" You are a physical being and living in a physical world - physical actions are part of the process. However, they are not the be all and the end all. You are a physical being living in a vibrational Universe. *The physical actions that you take will all have a vibration - an energetic alignment. What you attract will be based on a vibrational match.*

That is why your emotions are so important, by taking the action that feels the best, you are drawn to taking the action that is most a vibrational match, <u>at that moment in time</u>. Each moment is a fresh moment and the dynamics with you and the Universe are always changing. In another moment, another option may be better for you. The way you know is by how you feel in that moment, and so on.

Your life is a successive series of magical now moments. In each moment, you choose through your emotions what you are most resonant with.

112

The key thing is not the actions, but in lining up your vibration and following what is a vibrational match – you do that by following what feels best in that moment.

When you are a vibrational match to what you want, you will have the right ideas and inspiration to take the most appropriate actions - even no action, as appropriate - and the manifestations will happen in that respect. Actions are a part of the process, but not the be all and the end all. Vibration is what is most important if you want to be using Law of Attraction to attract in your life.

When you have vibrational alignment and are thinking and feeling from the place of having your goals and enJOYing them, you will be in the right place at the right time and doing and saying what you need to. You will be a channel for universal energy to flow through you for synchronicities and manifestations which are a win-win for all involved.

Sometimes, you may be better off not taking any actions. You will know this by following your feelings. If it feels better to be doing nothing, then at that moment, that is the right thing. *It is always about feeling from what you want and following your emotions in your moment.*

Many people tend to think that if they take no action then what they want will not happen. If you are a vibrational match, the Universe will bring you what you want. It is a metaphysical fact. It is Law. *The key thing is having thoughts and feelings and feeling from what you want and being a vibrational match – 'being' what you are wanting.* The actions are a part of the process in your alignment.

You are a physical being that will, in many cases, be attracting an outcome that is physical. So in likelihood the last step will be a physical step in your receiving and acquisition. It will be a natural step than one which is forced to 'make' it happen –

notice the difference in vibration in these two scenarios. One *where the physical attainment is a natural consequence of your vibration and you being you*, the other is using actions to 'make' or 'force' what you want to happen. With the latter there is an implication that you are not aligned and you need to be doing something to compensate for it.

Be present oriented and congruent with your now. What is most important is your energy in your now, than on what you are 'doing' necessarily. The doing will come as a natural consequence from your energy alignment.

It is important to be congruent and in alignment in your now. When you are taking action or doing something, be at peace with it and fine with whatever you choose to do. *The key thing is not the action that you choose, it is the vibrational alignment that you have.* If you are in conflict about it, then you are splitting your energy. The most important thing is your energetic alignment.

If you are worried about making mistakes or a mistake you have made previously, see it like a stream where that situation is gone and what is most important is your energy now. You cannot change what has gone before by looking back at it, but you can influence everything else by your attention and your energy here in your now. All possibilities and eventualities are from here, now. It's the only way.

114

Actions In Honing Your Vibration

Another part that action plays is in honing your vibration. You are living a physical life on a physical place, channelling universal energy through you. You are literally moulding your reality around you.

When you interact with your physical environment, you are shifting and changing your vibration constantly – everything is allowing you to expand, grow, and refine. This is another way that physical action can play a part in honing and refining your vibration to be in alignment with what you want. *By you doing and experiencing the things that are a match to what you want, you are creating that reality in your vibration in a very precise way.*

If you would like to own a certain car, then consider going to the showroom and seeing it. Look at the car, touch it, turn on the ignition, and hear it. Feel the interiors. Smell the upholstery or leather. If you are able to, take it for a test drive. Experience the car. Experience it in your neurology, your physiology, and your vibration. Experience it in a very real and vivid way (this can also be done with visualisation too if we are not able to experience something by being around it). *Make it that what you are experiencing now is an example of the way things will be. Use this experience to further practice your reality with this car.*

Similarly, if you are looking to purchase a home, find homes that are similar and look into them. *This is you sending a message to the Universe that you are congruent and aligned to what you want and ready to receive it and are doing the data gathering and experiencing to allow it in. This is a very real experience and so adds more power to your allowing of what you want.*

115

If you are looking to be in a relationship, interact with people of the opposite sex (or of the same sex) and be comfortable in their company. Use these experiences to be 'practising' your vibration and honing it.

Regardless of the eventuality of all of these situations, *know that you can never lose as your vibration has expanded and grown and is more refined as a result of the experiences that you have had.* This is always the case anyway, you are using specific situations to hone your vibration about those contexts or goals.

Notice how you feel as you experience the situations. Do you feel uncomfortable or negative? Or does it feel exciting and fun and positive? If it feels uncomfortable or negative then identify what about it is making you feel that way, and how you would like to be and feel instead and head towards that.

You are using these experiences to rehearse your reality. *By you experiencing it vibrationally, you are paving the ground for the physical reality of it.*

Everything happens in vibration before it comes into your physical reality.

Actions can play a part in making your vibration very real about what you want. The quickest, easiest, and most leveraged way can be through your thoughts, and certainly initially.

Through you entraining your abilities with your thoughts and emotions, you can imagine anything and as vividly as you like. As you do that and shift your vibration, the Universe will give you more examples and reinforcement. This will give you confirmation and further improve your expectation and

116

allowing, and the momentum builds and builds and soon enough you have your physical manifestations.

People Will Feel the Energy Behind Your Actions

It is the energy that you have behind an action that is more important than the action itself. It will define and contextualise the action itself.

When you do something from an energy of obligation, fear, or anything else that does not feel good, you are magnifying that energy by putting more attention to it, and reinforcing it with the action.

In general, people will be aware of it. They will most likely feel it, or at least that it is 'weak' energy, rather than something from a place of congruence, joy, alignment, love, and strength. They will be aware of it on a deeper level; whether they are aware of it consciously may or may not always be the case necessarily.

Most importantly, from your perspective, *it is about doing things from an energy that you want to attract more of the same energy.* Do things from a place of love and inspiration and joy, or whichever positive emotions, and attract more of the same.

It is never about the actions that you take but about the energy and the energetic alignment behind what you do.

117

The Physical Manifestations Are a Natural Consequence of Being You

Manifesting is about how you feel during the process; the manifestations themselves are natural consequences of your feelings.

People often come to want to learn manifesting and Law of Attraction in order to 'have' something, whether it be wealth or a relationship or whatever it may be that they want. They very much come with the attention on a possession or a 'thing' that they would like to have.

There is nothing wrong with having desires – that is what you are here for. You are here to have desires and expand and grow and bring them into your experience. *However, it is not about the 'things' that you acquire or the events that happen, it is about your expansion and growth and energetic and vibrational flow.*

You are a being of flow, not of acquisition. The acquisitions are a natural consequence of your flow, not the goal in itself. Your flow is what is important.

People often get caught up with and very attached to the things that they would like or the events that they would like to have happen, and do not remember what the process of manifesting and creating is really about.

Manifesting is not about the things, but about them indicating to you what is energetically important to you. It is using them as signposts and guidance as to what you want to flow energy towards. *The 'things' will tell you what is important to you and what isn't, by how you feel about them.*

The 'things' in the physical world are like a map of your energetic territory, they are not the territory themselves.

We get so caught up in our physical reality that we lose sense of who we really are, our spiritual and non-physical selves. *It is through our expression of who we are that we have the physical manifestations most easily.* It is through you *being* and consequently *feeling* that you *have*.

When your attention is on a possession or a thing that you would like, and you have a 'need' for it so that you can be happy, your attention is on something outside of you and not on the completeness that is within you.

It is through your awareness of your completion and delight in your now, that you attract more of the same and you attract manifestations that are a match.

And so that is why life can get difficult and some things (or people) can become so important to us because we 'depended' on them, and now "they have changed". Change is natural and constant. The reason it matters is not because they changed, but because of the meaning you put upon them, and how you are affecting *your* energy flow changes as a result of that meaning.

What is most important is your own connection to who you are. The things and people and experiences and events are indicators and signposts of that to you.

119

Love and Appreciation in Relationships

When two people come together, there is an immense love and appreciation for each other. Both are reflecting Source energy to each other and it feels exhilarating, wonderful, and so "alive" (That's how Source energy feels!). They are both flowing life energy to each other, vibrations are very high, and everything is possible.

Then sometimes what happens is there may be challenges along the way and attention to them creates resistance. The attention to the challenges creates attention to things with a negative emotion – resistance.

What happens then is either of the couple, or both of them, put their attention on the resistance and all of a sudden the flow of energy is not the same. They are resisting the flow of universal energy through themselves and to the other. This can be easily felt by either of them. The "alive" feeling that is not the same as it was.

Then what happens is the other person notices that they are not receiving the same affection from the other – they do not feel their connection to Source as the same - and they have an issue about it. They are then both blaming the other for the relationship when **what they did themselves was give the responsibility for their own Source connection to something (or someone) outside of themselves.**

Any time you forsake your own connection and put it through something or someone else, you are taking your own power away from yourself. This is not just power that you have, it is who you are.

120

And so that is why life can get difficult when some things (or people) can become so important to us because we 'depend' on them energetically. Then when "they have changed," we create discord in ourselves about it. We cannot keep people to be a certain way for the rest of their lives. *Change is natural and constant.*

The reason it matters is not because they have changed, but because of the meaning and significance you have put upon them, energetically, and how that is affecting your connection to Source. This is the same with anything that you have a relationship with or attention to. Whether it be a significant other, a child, parent, friend, mentor, teacher, passer by, a chemical or substance, an object – anything. It is to do with the reliance you place upon them, or it, for your flow of energy.

Addictions have been documented as such for their chemical 'fixes', but there are energetic reasons. The chemicals within something have an energy and it is the energy that one is addicted to. It is providing a temporary connection to Source. This is often why when someone tries to wean themselves off one item, they find something else to be addicted to. It is the energetic 'fix' that they are seeking.

When you see a picture of heaven in an object or thing or person, you may sometimes choose to seek more of that object or objects to find more of that heaven. All objects and experiences are only reflections of you. The heaven wasn't in the object, it was in you that was being reflected in that object.

WORKING WITH YOUR VIBRATION

Finding The Things That Feel Better

Your emotions are an indication of your vibration. They are an indication of your alignment with the larger non-physical aspect of you - 'You'.

The non-physical aspect of you knows all your desires vibrationally - they are all there in vibration, as well as the path to them. It is connected to infinite intelligence and All-There-Is. It communicates to you through your emotions. *The better you feel emotionally, the more in alignment your physical body is with the non-physical aspect of you.* The worst you feel, the more out of alignment that you are.

The key to using your vibration is finding and experiencing things that feel better and better to you. This will be a confirmation of you closing the gap between where you are physically, and where you are vibrationally non-physically.

You can be having thoughts that feel better, experiences that feel better, make choices that feel better, and so on. The thing to ask yourself is: "Is this improving my alignment with who I am?" And the way that you know that is by how it feels. If it feels better, you are improving your alignment and closer to what you want, and vice versa.

As your alignment increases – which is indicated by your emotions - you will also see the manifestations around you that are a match to your improved vibration. *You will be attracting better and better things into your life, and less of the things that were a match to the previous vibration.* The little things that used to frustrate you may be on their way out of your life.

When it comes to making decisions in your life, look for the things that feel the best. Get good at knowing what emotion you feel about different things and which feel better. At times it may define rational logic, but this information is from a far broader perspective than the rational logical perspective that you have from your physical eyes. *This information is from infinite intelligence which has a broader perspective.*

The non-physical aspect of you can see the path ahead and the route relative to where you are. It can see things that you cannot see from your physical perspective because you are too close to the trees, so to speak. Your emotions are the impulses of information being sent to you in every moment.

When people have desires and they set goals, many focus on the end results. They do not realise that *if they are wanting to manifest things in harmony with the Universe, it is their vibration - hence emotions - where their power is. It's to do with how your goals FEEL and creating that feeling place within you.*

Working with Negative Emotions

Sometimes, it may not be about finding something that feels good, it might be that you are experiencing negative emotions and it is about taking your attention off things that do not feel very good. Oftentimes it is easy to talk about feeling better and

124

better, but when we are going through experiences where there are negative emotions, it can feel very far away to think of feeling better.

The key then is to find things that feel less worse. It is about *soothing your emotions and finding things that feel less and less worse.* If you do this, you will quickly find your energy rising. Because you are no longer focusing on the things that create negative emotions within you, there is less resistance within you to universal energy and it can flow more freely into your life and through your body. Energetically, your body will feel this. You will also feel more energy to do certain things, and you may be seeing synchronicities begin to appear.

So if we are feeling negative, then it can be about finding things that feel less worse and getting yourself to a neutral point before you can start to consider things that feel better and better.

In freeing up the negative emotions, you are letting all that energy go and creating space for many new and fresh things to enter your life.

Milk the Emotions in Your Life

Whilst life can be about finding and following the things that feel the best, it can also be about finding things that feel even better in the choices that you have already made. It can be about *milking the positive emotions*.

Many people go through life, as they say, not smelling the roses. They try to be efficient and "get things done." This can be fine if it is in alignment. What we would like to suggest is to *enjoy the journey as well, if it feels better than the way that you have already been doing things.*

125

*As you increase the joy in your moments,
your moments of joy increase*

The Power in Realness and Specificity

We have already talked about focusing on things that feel better
as they are more in vibrational harmony with all that you are
wanting.

*As you focus more and more on the things that feel good
and that you enjoy, as you start to imagine them in your
life for real, the power behind them builds further.*

When you start to see yourself with what you want and imagine
it as real, it has great power. This is why people create vision
boards (collages or boards with images of the things that they
would like, that they can hang up, for example) or put posters
up, or write cheques in their name for very sizeable amounts to
put up on their wall, or photocopy their bank statements and
put large amounts for their account balance.

*These all serve to create a very real impression in their
mind of them having what they want.* This creates a very
precise, sharp and powerful vibration which is very attractive.

As you get more and more specific about what you would like,
this creates more pulling power. Remember that you came into
this physical plane to experience sharpness and focus. *By you
becoming more and more specific about what you want –
whilst keeping yourself in alignment, you are further
focusing your non-physical energy.*

126

The key is maintaining your alignment whilst getting specific. For some people, when they become specific about a certain outcome, they have beliefs and doubts that come up about them being able to have it. The thing to do then is to step back, be a bit more general about it and a bit softer about it, and regain alignment. Then, when it feels comfortable, to *continue being specific whilst it feels fun and enjoyable.*

Initially when you think of your goal, you may not be able to be specific. For example, when someone is wanting to attract a soulmate and they have not had much success, the first step for them could be just to state the intention that they would like someone. When I am working with a client on something like that, I would then get them to imagine that a bit more and gently add more details to this intention - whatever would naturally come up for them about it. As homework over the subsequent days, I would ask them to become more and more specific about what they are wanting.

What happens is as someone puts their attention around something, their familiarity with that vibration increases. As that familiarity increases, they will attract and allow other thoughts and find it easier and easier to focus on what they want and consider more things that are related to that vibration.

Natural inspiration occurs when you are in vibrational alignment with something. It may be divine inspiration, but it doesn't come out of nowhere. It comes from the alignment of your 'frequency', whether consciously or unconsciously.

It will get easier and easier for them to be more specific. In fact it may feel very natural. As they raise their vibration and shifting their perspective, they enable themselves to raise their vibration further and see other perspectives that serve them also.

127

In the example of wanting to attract a soulmate, initially they may have an intention. Upon focusing on this desire, very soon they will be able to be more specific and have an idea of certain characteristics, for example. They would then be more easily able to *imagine that and practice it in their mind as if it were a reality right now.*

The reason this happens is when anyone focuses upon something, you are practicing familiarity with that vibration. If you wanted to put it scientifically, you could also say you are honing and practicing your neurology to that thought. You are literally changing and rewiring your neurology.

In the coming days, this person would perhaps then be able to imagine scenarios of them going out to dinner with this soulmate, on holidays, and having happy experiences together, i.e. they are allowing and enabling a furthering of that line of thought that they are practicing.

These latter thoughts would not have been possible on the first day because it was a vibration that was too far away from where they were starting from initially.

Remember that you are a vibrational being and what we are talking about here is you building your vibration about what you want to be experiencing more of in your life. *It is about building familiarity with the vibrations that you want to experience, and enjoy.*

As you become more and more familiar with certain vibrations, you will see the manifestations of them more and more in your life.

As mentioned earlier in this book, *actions are another tool in honing your vibration and sending out a clear signal to the Universe.*

Do remember to take thoughts and vibrations of a contrary nature out of your consciousness. Take your attention away from the things that do not feel good. How do you do this? By how it feels. *If it feels uncomfortable or negative, turn your attention away and towards things that are more positive.* If you are in a context or situation where you cannot easily turn away at the time, *at least minimise your response and how you feel about it.*

It is not about what is in your reality. It is about your emotional reaction to what is in your reality. It is about how you feel. That's it. Change how you feel, and in time what is around you will change too.

Your desired physical manifestations will be getting closer to you as your vibrational (and energetic) signal gets clearer. It is all about you emitting a clear signal to the Universe and allowing what you want to come into your life.

What you want is ready to be in your life. It's about your allowing of it into your life by the signal that you give.

What Has Happened is a Part of Who You Are

When you have something which you do not want, on a deeper level - vibrationally - the seed is already set for what you DO want, it is a matter of aligning thoughts to let it come into your life

Everything that you experience adds to who you are on a vibrational level. You, along with the Universe are always expanding and growing.

You never contract, you are always expanding.

Anything that has ever happened never actually takes anything away from you or who you are - *you can never be less or be contracting in any way,* you only expand and grow on a vibrational level. Any experience, even a negative one, can *give you clarity about what you DO want.*

You are here in this physical playground to have physical experiences which give you diversity and highlight your preferences and desires. By your vibrational alignment to them, you bring these desires into your life. From these manifestations and new platforms that you create, you will make other choices and preferences of what else you would like and what you would like to expand further with, and so on.

When someone wants to be married, and they get into alignment with that desire and attract it into their lives, from the new platform, they have new perspectives. Perhaps they may like to go away together or have children together. These perspectives

130

are clearer and sharper from them being married than they might have been previously.

Everything that you experience is creating a platform for you to have new desires. It is all giving you new perspectives. You are in a stream of perspectives. You can choose what experiences and manifestations you would like to have in your life, and thus subsequent platforms to have new perspectives from.

If you have had a strongly negative experience, use that as clarity for what you DO want and what you would like to attract and align with and bring into your life and be living. Oftentimes what happens with people is when they have a negative experience they keep themselves in that place and vibrationally they attract more of the same and do not let in new things.

When people keep their focus and vibration on 'what was', they attract more experiences that are similar to 'what was'.

Someone could have come out of a relationship but be talking about the relationship that they came out of rather than the one that they would like to go into. And then they find that their next lover exhibits the same patterns of the previous relationship. Or they may find that their relationship with their employer takes a turn for the worse commensurate with the vibration that they have been offering from their previous relationship. *Nothing enters your life or your experience without being a vibrational match on some level.*

Wherever you go, there you are...

131

Some people move countries. They move countries to start a new life but they give off the same vibration as they were in the previous country by putting their attention and emotions towards the same things and attracting similar situations in a whole new environment.

It is not the situations or circumstances that determine your life, it is your vibration - which is from your focus and attention. What you attract will be a match to the frequency you offer, whether deliberate or unintentional, conscious or unconscious.

Going from Problem to Solution

Take what happens to you in your life as a gift and use it to direct your focus and attention towards what you would like, and how you would like things to be. *Your greatest power is in being able to change your perspective about anything in your experience*.

When you are presented with a challenge or a 'problem', shift your attention to how you would like things to be. The reason that sometimes this is not so easy, especially in the immediacy of experiencing a perceived problem, is due to the emotions involved. They can be shock, fear, anger, guilt, and other factors. No wonder it can be difficult focusing on the solution with all that 'noise'!

As you gently sooth those emotions and move towards a focus of how you would like things to be, your vibration shifts. As this happens, the things around you also change, and it becomes easier. Then, *the momentum builds and it is easier to focus on how you would like things to be because what is happening around you is also reflecting it more and more.*

132

The Universe can only bring you your solution when you take your attention off the problem. If your attention is fixated on what is wrong, and that is the vibration that you are offering, how can a solution enter your life?

This is why it is often said that "letting go" can be useful. What you are doing is *letting go of the problem and creating space for the solution to enter.* Sometimes you may not know what the solution is or even have thought about it, but just by letting go of the problem, you are creating space for the solution. And soon enough, before you know it, something synchronistic occurs and it has resolved itself.

Emotions

Emotions are what orient our attention. It is not necessarily 'what' you are thinking, but the emotions behind what you are thinking that provide the energetic momentum.

This is why often you may try not to think about something, but if you are having an underlying emotion about it, it keeps coming up in your thoughts. You may be 'trying' not to think about it, but there is an underlying emotion that is keeping it in your consciousness..

The key thing with any issue is to identify the emotions. It makes it a lot easier when you have identified them, rather than being in them and not being aware of them.

Sometimes people will say that living from the heart can be painful and it is easier to live from the mind and logic. Think about that statement. If something is 'painful', it is already a decision from the heart. So that statement about following logic would in itself be a decision from the heart.

The Non-Physical World Around You

Whilst you see a physical world, there is also a non-physical or a spiritual aspect to it which is so much more. It is a *so much broader and expanded version of the physical world around you.*

Everything that you see around you, including the physical objects, the people, the animals - everything - has a non-physical unseen equivalent to it.

Just as you see a physical world, it is blended with a non-physical and spiritual world. The physical manifestations you see around you are a blending of the physical and non-physical. Most people have only been aware of what is so easy to see – the physical.

The non-physical is vibrating at a different frequency but is everywhere. In fact it is a deeper aspect of the physical. Much like you have an iceberg where you see the top one eighth or so of it and you have an underlying larger and dominant proportion that is unseen. *The physical is an extension of the non-physical.*

There is a broader perspective to what you have been so used to only seeing. And in your awareness of this now, and as you continue through this book and harmonise and align to this, possibilities open up for you. *You will find yourself in more and more of a rhythm with things around you and more in harmony and you will experience more and more synchronicities.*

It will not be unusual for you to wake up and find things happen in your day that take care of themselves. That you will have known how to set your intent and your vibrational expectation for that day and things to orchestrate themselves.

You will be setting the course of your ship and finding yourself in the beautiful clear blue waters and with a beaming sun looking down on you. There may be times where the waters get choppy and in those moments you will have clarity in setting your course.

In you being aware of this larger, broader aspect of the world around you, along with what you will learn later in this book, you will start to understand why things happen the way they do in the world around you. You will have answers to many of the questions you have asked yourself over the years, and you will have a deeper understanding of everything.

As You Become Aware of Your Broader Perspective, You See Everything Differently

Whilst you see the physical body that you are so familiar with, *there is a larger spiritual and non-physical part of you that is the essence and 'spirit' for this physical body.*

This is why when people have tried to solve things by focusing only on the physical world causes, they may not always have had lasting change – because the physical world is not *all* there is.

135

Just as when you see an iceberg, the greater part of it is beneath the surface. The same is true for you too. There is much more than the physical person you see. *You are spirit manifest in physical form. You are connected to all there is on a deeper level and all possibilities are open to you.*

There is a magic within you, and when you know it, you will see it everywhere.

MANIFESTING: TAKING SOMETHING FROM THE UNSEEN TO THE SEEN

Manifesting is taking something from the unseen to the seen. It already exists. Everything already exists. Everything that you have thought already exists. By your attention and focus to them, you are bringing those most believed and resonant into your physical reality.

'Manifesting' is something you have been doing ALL your life – and before your life too! You could not have existed if you did not. **Your physical presence is a manifestation itself in this world.**

We have always been manifesting things. In fact, everything is a manifestation. It's just whether you have manifested the things that you want or not.

You are in a constant flow with the Universe, engaged in an energetic dance. You are constantly manifesting. The question is, are your beliefs enabling you to allow the manifestations that you are wanting into your life?

When you have a desire - when you have a thought of something that feels good - the Universe knows what you want. But if your vibration contradicts it then what you want cannot enter your life.

The Path of Least Resistance

When water flows along the stream, it will do so via the path of least resistance. It does not look for the hardest and longest away to find its way to where it wants to go - this is against natural flow.

I recently did a Law of Attraction seminar in Las Vegas where I talked about the "Path of Least Resistance":

The Universe will always get to you what you want the easiest way it can - via the path of least resistance. Your beliefs and thoughts – which influence your vibration - determine the path of least resistance in your 'allowing' of it.

What you want can only come to you the easiest way it can based upon how your beliefs allow it to get to you. If you have beliefs that prevent you believing it can be in your life or that you are better off not having it in your life, you will make it harder for you to experience it.

Some thoughts to consider:
- What do you believe about what you want?
- Is it ok for you to have it, right now?
- How would it feel for you to have it right now?
- How easy is it for you to have what you want?
- Is it possible to you to have what you want?
- What consequences, if any, do you believe there are in having what you want?

Remember, the above will highlight your beliefs. It does not mean that is the way that things are, *it is how you are believing that they are based on your present beliefs.*

When the student is ready the teacher will appear.
Are you ready for what you are looking for?

Abundance, like anything else, will find its way to you via the path of least resistance. The infinite flow of the Universe flows to you and through you. *How much of it you let into your experience is based on your thoughts and beliefs - vibration.*

When you have thoughts and beliefs which are contrary to what you want you are 'resisting' your natural flow in having what you want. And of course, if your beliefs are not set up for you to allow or let into your experience what you want, then you could have the most amazing and infinite and abundant Universe - which you do - but no way of having what you want in your experience because the signals you are sending out are for something else.

What comes to you in your life will be in the easiest way it can enter your life, based upon your beliefs about it.

It is like there is a whole spectrum of radio stations and you are tuning into the one which is playing what you do not want because that is what you are paying your attention to. Adjust your signal.

139

FEEL and think and be from what you want.
Experience it as here. Be the embodiment of it.
Be the living vibration of it.

Allow your beliefs to enable the things that you want into your life. When you practice the thoughts and the vibration of what you want and become more and more of a vibrational match to what you want, you are making it easier for it to enter your life. You are getting into resonance and frequency with what you want.

What you want cannot not enter your life if you are a vibrational match to it, it is metaphysical law.

One way that we do not support our natural flow is when we impose upon the Universe how it should bring what we want into our lives. Remember, it's about the path of least resistance. It's about your openness and allowing of possibilities. The Universe has many more possibilities than those you may be consciously aware of. You do not need to know them or the 'how', but in you being allowing and open to them, you can be receptive to them.

The Universe can bring you what you want via an infinite number of ways. The way it will come to you is via the ways that you are more receptive to, or least resistant to.

We often get occupied with the 'means' of how we want what we want to enter our lives. *Instead, focus on WHAT you want and even WHY you want it - what it will mean for you, what will happen etc - let go of the 'how'.* You will be focusing on the vibrational aspects of what you want and letting the Universe organise the 'how'.

When you are a vibrational match to what you want, the 'How' will take care of itself. You become a vibrational match by putting your thoughts and feelings – your dominant vibration - on what you want. The Universe has an infinite number of ways of bringing you what you want - don't limit it by imposing your beliefs on how it should bring it to you.

'Need' Can Imply Focus on Absence or Lack on Some Level

One indication that we are acting from a place of lack is by how something feels. If we feel we are chasing or not feeling balanced or aligned then it is likely to be from that place. If we are expressing from a place of love and it feels good and inspired, then we are likely to be in a good place and attracting what we want

If you feel you are 'chasing' things, it can be from a place of lack. Are you after it because you are lacking in your now in some way? Or because you are complete and whole and having this thing is just another natural expression of who you are?

We are not saying do not desire things or go after them. Just be conscious of the desire and the motivation (which make up your vibration) about what you want. If it is from a place of incompleteness, you may be emanating that.

Sometimes we may have beliefs that we need to take actions and we then allow ourselves to feel complete. The key thing is, however you get to it, ideally *be from your place of completeness, of 'beingness' of what you want, and make the manifestation of it a natural consequence.*

Allow yourself to feel and follow what inspires you and brings you alive. Love your moment and be in the flow.

'Need' can imply a focus on absence or lack on some level. At the least it implies attachment. The attention to lack can be from a place of if we don't get what we 'need' then we are 'without' – hence an element of lack.

Any time we have attention to what we do not want in our vibration, we are not letting in or allowing what we want as easily as we can.

Ask yourself, what would happen if you didn't have this? Is it a "need to" or "have to"? What would happen if you didn't have it? What is the feeling that you get? If it is an uncomfortable feeling, then on some level there is an attention to lack. Take this as feedback and align and adjust towards what you DO want. What would you like instead? How would you like things to be?

Rather than having all your hopes resting on the completion or on the goal, put your attention on the enjoyment of the process of the manifestation

When you have all your hopes resting on the completion of a goal, you are likely to be in a place of 'need' and perhaps even fearful that it may not work out for you. This does not necessarily need to be the case. *You can have your full attention on the total joy and delight of something, regardless of how it shows up or if it does.*

You may perceive the goal or outcome to be your only hope for some reason, but you do not need to give your attention to that. Put your attention on the delight of it. In doing so, you are increasing your chances and probabilities of success rather than it being from a place of fear and trepidation.

If you are vibrationally in the right place, the 'right' things will take care of themselves

Of course, everything is from a place of relativity. You may be someone at this moment in time who uses fear to motivate themselves and for you it may be fine doing it that way. In the long run I would suggest focusing on vibrations that feel better and better. If you are using fear to motivate yourself, there is attention – and hence vibration – to what you do not want (i.e. something that you are fearing and moving away from) on some level.

Some people use negative emotions to motivate themselves. Whilst that serves a function and a purpose, overall in the long-term, I would suggest orienting towards emotions that feel better. *They will be kinder on your body, they will feel better, you may find that more things happen around you synchronistically or quicker, and in likelihood that you have to make less 'effort'.*

143

What You Want Already Exists

The moment you have a thought about something, it is in vibration. The precursor to the thought itself is a vibrational momentum that led to that thought.

The reason the physical manifestation of your thought hasn't entered your physical experience yet is because you are not the same vibration as it yet, you are not yet offering the same frequency. Through your positive feel-good attention to it, you are pulling it into your experience and you are coming together and you are attracting more of the same, and it is just a matter of time. I emphasise "positive feel-good attention" because if you are focusing on the lack of it, you are pushing it away and attracting the lack of it.

What you want is already created on the non-physical. You are bringing that into physical manifestation by your thoughts about it.

The process of alignment and of tweaking and adjusting your thoughts to FEEL and BE from the same place as what you want is what closes the gap between the two of you. *Your emotions serve as guidance and as an indicator as to how close you are to what you want.*

Follow what feels better. Follow what feels lighter. Follow your inspiration. Turn away from things that feel heavy and things that bog you down. Follow the things that light you up. These are all indications to things that you are more in alignment with.

In following what feels better – which is communication from the deeper part of you - you are closing the gap between where you are on a physical level, and where you are on a non-physical.

The non-physical 'you' is already where you want to be. The physical 'you' is yet to be there. But you will close the gap by following what feels best and doing that in each moment.

When you chose to come into this life, you chose the best experiences in line with what you are asking for on a vibrational level. You chose the 'details' that would create the experiences that you wanted to experience.

Just as you physically manifest things in your life, *your physical body is a manifestation of your spirit and vibration.* There is also no coincidence in the people that are in your life, they are ALL vibrational matches. There are no coincidences. There are attractions of like-frequencies.

In realising that everything is vibration and thought, you can see that what you want - which is initially in thought and intention - and the actual physical manifestation of it, are no different.

Your desire for what you want contains the mechanics of 'how' to have it, just like in every seed is the mechanics of the growing of a tree.

LOVE, YOU, AND THE UNIVERSE

True love is open to you as quickly as your ability to be open to it...

Love is one of the most keenly asked about topics (Money is another, and we have already talked about abundance!). Why is it such an important topic?

It can be said that love is predominant everywhere in the Universe. Not necessarily just a romantic love, but an energy, an affection, an interconnectedness, and much, much more. Some would say that 'love' binds everything together.

I would say that *everything is about energy, vibration, and love itself is an energy and a vibration.*

Love is an Indicator of Your Relationship to Who You Are

The reason that love is so important to so many is because often *love is the surface level word that people are aware of that is an indication of their connectedness to who they are* – to the aspect of them which is non-physical or spiritual.

The energetic or spiritual aspect of a person being that which the body is a physical extension of. That which is so much more than the physical body and 'who' you really are. *When we feel love, it is an indicator of the alignment of our thoughts, actions and more – our vibration – to 'who' we are.* What

147

we feel for another is an expression and a 'projection' of something that we feel within us.

When someone falls in love, that feeling of love is an indicator of their connectedness of who they are - to the non-physical aspect of themselves - than an indicator just of that romantic relationship.

The romantic relationship is something that has enabled this person to be more connected to who they are. It is always about your connection to who you are. What leads you to it is a tool, a signpost, a guide, and not the be all and end all. *What is most important is your relationship to yourself –* that larger non-physical aspect of you. *All other relationships...in fact everything else, is an expression of it.*

You are living this physical life as an expression of the relationship between your physical body and the larger non-physical spiritual aspect of you. The world you experience is as a result of that relationship. You cannot try to fix all other relationships in the world without affecting this one. Improve this relationship, and you improve all others in your world too.

The Feel-Good Emotions are
An Indication of Your Connection

When someone goes into a relationship, they experience a beautiful love and appreciation being flowed at them by the other person - they are having Source energy (from the source of all creation) being shone upon them. This is beautiful and

148

amongst the most exhilarating feelings ever. In turn, they most likely reciprocate and there is a beautiful flowing of energy.

What happens often is that it is assumed that the good feelings are just because of the other person. *In actuality, the feelings are an indication of your connection to who you are which has been triggered, and reflected, by what you have been experiencing.*

Oftentimes we get caught up in the illusion that's ahead of us, that we forget about the relationship that's within us.

The emotions are not *because* of what has been sent to you by the other person, though instead because of the connection that you have to who you are. *What happened is the affection shown to you by another has been a trigger, and reflection, to your connection to who you are.*

The rest of the Universe serves to remind you of your connection to who you are. People chase the rest of the Universe, but it starts with what's within. When you find alignment – by what feels good – everything in the rest of your Universe changes for you.

When Someone Keeps Attracting The Wrong Relationship

Relationships, like everything else, are contexts where you are reflecting yourself. It may not always be easy to assume or imagine, but *what you experience - as with the rest of your life -is a reflection of yourself and your vibration.*

149

When someone has been in a relationship which has not worked for them and they are unhappy, they may choose to end the relationship and move on. What sometimes happens is that when the person goes into another relationship, they – by their focus – can still be carrying the same vibration from the end of the previous one, which isn't helpful.

You may change scenery, relationships, jobs, countries and more; what stays with you is your vibration. Change your focus and vibrational offering and what is around you will change, or you will attract a change. Either way, it will be a match to your frequency.

By being present moment oriented, or future-intention oriented, you can take your attention away from the past and towards something that feels better. It does not matter so much where your attention is - in terms of the past, present and future - *it is more important that your attention is on something that is offering a vibration of what you want to be having more of.* Be aware of your emotional offering.

The Universe is not listening to your words, it is listening to the vibration that you are offering. That is the language of the Universe.

The Experiences On The Outside Are Symbols Of Who YOU Are

The relationship that you will ALWAYS have is with the non-physical – or spiritual - aspect of you. It is who you are; who you are as a physical being is an extension of it.

150

Understandably, when we are living physical lives and are very used to them, we assume that what happens in the physical world is all there is. What we do not realise is that what happens on a physical level is a reflection of who we are on a non-physical, or spiritual, level. *We are physical reflections of the beautiful spirits that we are.*

In a sense, the physical world is a playground which is reflecting who you are – what you see and experience is an echo of your vibration. You respond to these reflections and make choices and decisions which alter your vibration, and lead to subsequent 'platforms' and paths in your experience.

The physical plane is so very real – as it is meant to be. Our experiences, emotions, and reactions to it are very real, focused and powerful - and we assume that it is all there is. We assume that the bright shiny objects that we experience in the world are all there is. *In actual fact, the bright shiny objects are a reflection and a magnification of what is already within us.* They wouldn't show up in our experience if they didn't already exist within us.

Love is something that you experience on the outside which is a magnification of what is on the inside.

When someone is going from relationship to relationship or experience to experience, this can be very difficult for them as it may feel like they are dealing with 'moving targets' as they go from one situation to another. Realise that *what is within you is the true constant.* It is not moving. *Change what is*

151

within you, and you change what will be reflected on the outside.

It is easier when you realise that the world within is *your* world and you can play with it and change it how you see fit. The moving targets on the outside can be distracting because they are the *symbols and expressions* of who you are rather than who you are. ***They are the reflection, not the source.***

Use what you experience as an indication to reveal YOU

Your 'Soulmate' is a Reflection of You

In one respect, it could be said that **everything and everyone that you experience is your 'soulmate' because you are all aspects of the same 'soul'**, of the same larger whole. Also, anything and everything that you come into contact with will be a vibrational match, otherwise they would not be in your physical experience. If you were vibrational opposites, you would be in different places.

Of course, this does not mean that we want to be getting into a 'soulmate' romantic relationship with everyone that we experience! Just that we can have an awareness that **we are matches, that's why we have shared the same physical time-space experience.**

The reason that meeting a soulmate is so highly desired by people – and usually outside of their conscious awareness - is because they are looking to meet something in this Universe (i.e. a person in this case) which is a strong vibrational match to who they are, and where they are at, vibrationally.

They do not often consciously know this, but they are following their emotions, unconsciously usually, though perhaps being aware of actions in their conscious awareness. *Implicit in following these emotions is the connection to who they themselves are.*

Love is one of those most desired of experiences because of how we perceive it. And how we perceive it is because of what it means to us. *When we feel love, it is one of the strongest connections and confirmations that we are a match to who we are on a deeper level.* It is just we assume that the other person is what our emotions are about, when in fact they have served to *remind us how we feel about ourselves.*

For those that are seeking 'soulmates', *by changing how they see themselves and feel about themselves, they change what and who comes into their life.* People tend to look to the 'outside' for answers. That is just the reflection. *You have to work with the source, which is you and your inner world.*

The physical world can be seen like a very real illusion that is a projection of your relationship with yourself. Change the vibration, the world changes.

How we feel as a result of someone loving and appreciating us can only be experienced by us if on some level we feel that about ourselves. *What we experience in our lives with the physical world serves to illuminate and remind us of our relationship with ourselves, or rather, our Self.*

Find You, and You Find Everything

You Do Not Need Another To Complete You

You are whole and complete and in your realisation of your completeness, you will attract another.

When you feel that someone needs to 'complete you', you are creating a dynamic with lack. In your perception that you need to be complete, you will attract confirmation of your incompleteness. Instead, realise that *in this now moment, you are as complete as you can be*, and be open to what is a match to that.

If you are living your life requiring someone else or something else to complete you, if that implies that you are lacking in some way in your now, you are offering that vibration and will attract experiences that confirm your incompleteness.

That 'incompleteness' is a perspective. *You are actually totally and wholly complete in this moment.* There is nothing that you need other than what is in your now for you to be totally complete. Shed away any perception that something is required to make you whole. *Any perception of incompleteness is an illusion.*

Any perception to any lack is an illusion. It is a distortion of the infinite and abundant possibilities. *The Universe is an abundant place, and the perception of lack is one possible way of perceiving it. It is one way of perceiving it if you choose to, but it is not the way the Universe is.* The Universe will even create an abundance of lack if you so choose.

154

Let's say you are someone that is financially challenged at this moment and you believe that you require money to complete you. Change that perspective so that you **realise that you are complete in so many ways**. Take your attention away from the perception of incompleteness around the notion of money or love, or anything else.

If you think about it, perhaps you are financially challenged *because* of your beliefs about being incomplete about money right now. **Change your beliefs and see what happens**, and *really* believe it, not just for the sake of it. See what that leads you towards or what that enables you to see so that you can make other changes.

Should I Find Another Relationship or Make The Most Of This One?

If someone is in a relationship and it's not quite working out how they would like it to, should they find another relationship or make the most of the one they are in?

Firstly, remember that you may change your environment but you always take your vibration with you. **If you change your environment but are thinking the same thoughts and feeling the same emotions, you will be offering the same vibration and soon enough that environment will match your vibration.**

The answer really lies in the path of least resistance. Which is the easiest path? It may be easy to leave a relationship, but then you may still have to do the vibrational work to deal with whatever the cause of the issue was in the first place so that you do not attract it in the next relationship.

155

Or, you could carry on with life and see what happens next time and let Law of Attraction let you know where you are at vibrationally, rather than tuning in to your feelings and emotions about the context of relationships.

You can never get it wrong as **whatever you do in life, Law of Attraction will attract more of the same. It will reflect whatever your vibration is to you.** If there is anything that you need to be aware of, you will find out in time and can then reorient your focus and vibration towards how you want things to be.

You can wait for the manifestations to happen to give you tangible evidence, or you can tune in to your emotions and vibration in how you feel about something to change your direction, if you need to, pre-manifestation.

If you choose to make the most of the current relationship, how do you do so? When people are in relationships and there are small problems, what happens with time (and focus!) is these problems build and grow into larger issues. Ideally, the thing to do is to **step away from these issues and start with a clean, fresh slate.**

If two people in a relationship can see themselves each day as new lovers, they have the makings of a romance of a lifetime.

Sometimes, because of people's beliefs, they may feel they need to 'work' through these issues than walking away from them. Individual beliefs about how they allow themselves to gain peace on an issue can be respected.

156

But that is what it is about – **allowing oneself to be at peace with something and moving on.** If they are not at peace with the issue and keep bringing it up or thinking about it and offering a vibration about it, the problem is likely to continue. **The solution is to take that problem – or the emotions that caused it – out of their vibration.**

If someone has a particular problem, identify the emotions and thoughts behind it. What are they feeling? Why? What does it remind them of? Is it to do with self worth? Fear? Anger? Then it is to release these emotions if they feel they need to, but **more importantly, put their focus on something else. This can be either by getting at peace with that issue, or thinking about things that feel better.**

How did it feel when they first fell in love with their partner? What was their first date like? Their first kiss? What is it their partner does that makes them melt? What do they love doing for their partner? Notice that all of these are likely to create a positive vibration within the person, **if they allow themselves to.** And this is the key thing.

When we have a disagreement with someone, we can carry the remnants of that disagreement far beyond the actual moment of the disagreement itself. You are ready to move on right away, but if you keep going back to that event in your thoughts, you are not allowing yourself to move on and offer a new, fresh vibration.

You are usually ready to move on from an issue right away. But it is through your attachment to the situation with your emotions that you do not let yourself move on.

Realise that the holding on to the emotion is damaging and destructive not only to that particular relationship, but to

157

yourself also. When you create resistance within yourself - which is what all negative emotion does - you create the platform for more negative emotions as you are getting more and more into that frequency. You are also blocking your natural, abundant, infinite well-being.

The overall solution is to *allow yourself to make peace with the situation – for yourself. You can only ever do things for yourself; whether it benefits another will be up to their allowing of it.* And that is their job, so to speak.

When you do a favour for another, it is up to their receptivity as to how much of that favour they allow into their experience. Some will be grateful and appreciative, others will not. You focus on the joy of your giving; the rest is up to them.

Regarding disagreements, your job is to allow yourself to move on from it vibrationally. If others do or do not, that is down to their allowing. Whether you communicate further and work with *their* allowing of a better vibration within themselves is up to you, but *your greatest influence is when you have first made the change within yourself.*

Allow yourself to move on from the particular situation and the vibration of it to disappear down the infinite universal stream and focus your attention on new fresh 'water' in this universal stream, so to speak. *Orient yourself towards how you would like things to be and the things that feel good. And soon enough, you will see these into your reality more and more.*

Sometimes, you may have changed focus yet still be experiencing situations which are not pleasant. These may just be remnants which are leaving your physical reality and allowing new, positive and fresh experiences to come in. *Keep your focus on what feels good and allow those things not wanted to disappear.*

When we are having our attention on what we do not want, that is creating 'noise' within us and attention, time, focus, and energy away from how we want things to be.

If by these 'remnants' appearing you start to think that you have not moved on and put your attention on these unpleasant situations, you are putting your vibration back on what you do not want and are allowing yourself to be more receptive to more of it.

Always, always have your vibration on what feels good to you and in the emotional range of where you want to be. In the case of relationships, remind yourself what you adore and appreciate in the other. As you start to put your attention there, you attract more of the same, and that builds and grows.

If you want to experience love, offer the vibration of love within yourself. Be the Source for the Universe to reflect to.

The Universe has Soulmate after Soulmate For You

Attraction is two spirits meeting each other and using physical criteria, amongst others, to rationalise their attraction. We experience and recognise vibration first and foremost – all other senses are a re-presentation from that

159

When you think of your soulmate, what are the essences that you feel? Love? Joy? Happiness? Ecstasy? What else? *Make these more and more a part of your experience and what you feel on a daily basis.*

On your journey, as you raise your vibration, you will find that who and what you attract into your life will change as a reflection of that.

Also, *take your attention away from what is missing in your life.* Take your attention away from the fact that you do not yet have your soulmate in your physical presence just yet, if that is the case. It is ok if for a moment you consider these things to set your attention for what you *do* want, but do not dwell or keep your attention around what is missing.

If you are offering the vibration of lack, what you want could be right next to you but you would not see it because your eyes are looking for something else.

Ask yourself what your beliefs are about having your soulmate or partner in your life, or with whatever words you use to describe this area of your life. Are you fine to have this person in your life right now? Or do you feel in some respects you're not ready or worthy to have this? If so, identify these beliefs and resolve them. *They are all illusions that create a separation from allowing you to have what is yours right now.*

What beliefs to you have about being able to meet someone that is a match for you? *Do you feel it can happen?* Or do you feel that it is a rare thing? *Realise that the Universe will reflect your beliefs. If you believe so (or at least have an*

160

openness and an absence of doubt), it will find soulmate after soulmate after soulmate for you - if you believe so.

Remember, everything is energy and vibration. Through your thoughts, you have the power to mould and shape the world and reality around you.

Also ask yourself, is your life on hold waiting for this soulmate? Are you withholding happiness from yourself in your now because of something that you are 'waiting' for? *If you are withholding something from yourself, you are offering that vibration and the Universe corresponds also – it gives you reasons to continue waiting, until you feel you are ready.* Allow yourself to live and bask in your wholeness right now, and let the Universe reflect that back to you.

'Self Love' is an Allowing of Who You Are

'Self love' is an allowing of who you are. It is not an arrogance or a delusion, it is a natural <u>allowing</u> of who you are. 'Allowing' often means not disallowing. It can be seen as the allowing of the essence, the spirit, the non-physical nature of who you are. The indication of it, is that you feel good.

For some, self love has become important for them because they have been practicing self denial in many cases. They have taken treatment from others which was not very nice and for them "self love" is the antithesis and part of the journey to experiencing pure love for themselves. Their journey may be

161

starting from a place which is not very positive. In releasing some of the negative conditioning that might be there, such as low self esteem, they are opening and 'allowing' who they are.

Initially for them it will have the vibration of the denial of love that they experienced and that is part of their journey. It is a vibration of moving away from something, but at least they are on their way and in the right direction.

When you think and flow love and appreciation, you are naturally experiencing love through you and offering the vibration of it. You are a channel for the Universe's love.

Delight, appreciation and enjoyment of your now are ways that you maximise your presence in your now. Anytime you are doing that, you are filling your now with your being.

If you are in a state of ecstasy, love or joy, you will be flowing beautiful feeling energy. You are allowing your beautiful spirit to flow through you and are a match to things of a similar vibration.

Unconditional Love is Something You Allow Yourself

Unconditional love is taking away requirements and conditions to experience and give love. Experiencing and giving love are two aspects of the same whole. *When you release conditions from others having to be a certain way, you also release conditions in you feeling a certain way.*

In you releasing conditions for another to be a certain way, you are actually releasing conditions upon yourself. You thought you were releasing another, but the prisoner was always you.

Expressing and experiencing unconditional love is something you really do for yourself more than for someone else. Your relationship with the Universe is actually through your relationship with yourself; there is no separation in that respect. *When you allow yourself unconditional love and are kinder to yourself, you express that to everything else through you also.*

When you feel better within you, you feel better about everything else also. Remember, everything else is a reflection from within you. When you change the source, you change the reflection.

It will always be about your relationship with yourself – your Self. All relationships you have externally are always expressions of your relationship with yourself.

It is about not allowing *yourself* to take yourself out of *your* flow for what others do. Find and look for the things that feel the best to you, because that is what is best *for you*. In turn, the Universe is better for it too.

Through your alignment to yourself and your best feeling emotions, you create vibrational pathways for others. Through your path to your Self, you serve as a shining example and inspiration to others. There is nothing more valuable you can offer them than that.

COMPILATION OF SOME OF HEMAL RADIA'S QUOTES

Exclusive to this version

"No dream is given to you without the means to attain it"

"Love sees no age, colour or judgement, it connects deeply within, person to person, soul to soul"

"The depth of any sea, the peak of any mountain, the far flung edge of the Universe, none of these are impossibilities for you, just a matter of time, focus, and application. You always get there in the end. No goal is out of reach for you. Your beliefs about it determine how quickly and how it comes. LIVE with the expectation that it is yours and you have claimed it, undeniably. Let the Universe respond to your faith about it."

"Let the experiences of your life be like the petals upon a flower, each one adding to, enriching and shaping the beautiful being that is you..."

"To have a 'soulmate' relationship, it helps to have found your own 'soul'"

"When I realised what you meant to me, what everything else meant to me changed too"

"Another moment with you is another pearl of love surrounding my heart"

"The greatest gift you can give another is yourself. You cannot give that gift if you are being someone else to be with them."

"Know that no one can truly take anything away from you when you are comfortable in realising who you really are"

"When you love truly from your soul, there is no risk you can ever take. It's about your love, not the other person."

"When you are 'being' something, whether it's in physical yet or not, you are offering the vibration of it. Someone, for example, is a 'mother' long before they are pregnant. The conception is a natural consequence of their 'being'. Things happen in vibration and on an unseen level before they happen on a physical level."

"The Universe is a beautiful place. Fears and other negative emotions occur when you are not seeing it for what it fully is, you are seeing it as limited in some way. It's actually a place that loves and adores you and is on your side."

"You came together to love and adore each other, not to be scared of what the future may hold"

"Allow yourself to see yourself in the best way. There will be those that resonate and want to share in that reality, and there will be those that don't. Allow yourself to be around those that want to share in that reality.

"One of the easiest ways to get to where you want to be is to be able to appreciate where you are"

"The Universe doesn't make mistakes. You are here for a reason."

"When you move out of or away from things, remember to look forward not back"

"There is only one true love affair; the one with yourself. All others are expressions of it."

"Have you noticed that as you are getting to know someone, as you are getting closer, sometimes it might appear that the differences get bigger? Realise that there are also similarities there that can be accentuated, nurtured and grown. Take responsibility for what you focus on in the other person."

167

"There are no defeats, endings or losses, there are only transitions"

"The only broken dreams are those that you stop dreaming"

"People, resources, synchronicities will all be organized in perfect harmony by the Universe matching your vibration"

"The Universe will give you a match to your beliefs. If you believe/expect your desires come with consequences, it will comply. If you believe you can have your desires and be very happy, it will comply."

"As you shine a light in your abundance, you become an inspiration for others to theirs. Also in your own abundance, the Universe expands and there is more for everyone."

"Every cell in your body is responding to your vibration. When you set your vibrational tone, every cell responds to it."

"The better we get at liking where we are at, the better where we are at becomes"

"Look for the gifts in each moment"

"Possibilities grow as you practice looking for them..."

"What lies ahead of you starts within you"

"The softest touch can be the strongest,
the lightest touch can be the deepest"

"When you focus on the magic in the person in front of you, the
'differences' in your mind can disappear because you are busy focusing
on the magic. Focus on the love, not on the gap.
What you focus on, expands."

"The Universe sees through all masks.
Might as well be who you are..."

"You are freer and have more possibilities in this Universe than you
may realise. You have the power to change your thoughts and change
the signal to the rest of the Universe.
What more power than that would you want?"

"Let go of the 'how' - focus on what you want and what feels good to
you about it, such as 'why' you want it.
Let the 'how' reveal itself to you."

"In each moment, we are writing our story, and it is only limited by
what we dare to write"

"You never truly lose in anything. You win every time, vibrationally, in everything you do. You have perspectives and choices EVERY time that you did not have before. You are RICHER for all you experience and in getting to experience an aspect of this Universe in all you do."

"There is no limit to the love your heart can hold nor to the love that can flow through it. Try it..."

"Unconditional love starts with unconditional love for you"

"Your emotions know the path of least resistance — the shortest path to where you want to be. Use them as guidance."

"The light you hold within you is far brighter than any darkness you can imagine"

"There is no voice as loud as the calling of your soul for the path that is ahead for you"

"When you are in a place of love, the Universe beats a path to your door to make it all happen"

"Tomorrow always comes sooner when we enjoy today"